Praise for *Beyond the Surface*

"A deeply moving, inspiring, and heart-opening call to action that illuminates how self-acceptance is possible and essential for every single one of us. Amidst our epidemic of not-enoughness, Jessica's book shines as a bright light of actionable hope."

NATALY KOGAN

author of *Happier Now* and *The Awesome Human Project*

"It's been said that the best writing 'makes the personal universal.' By bringing us into her story, mind, and heart, Jessica Long achieves this with flying colors. *Beyond the Surface* is a rallying cry to show up for yourself, your dreams, and your world—and will fire you up to do just that."

KATIE HORWITCH

founder of WANT: Women Against Negative Talk and author of *Want Your Self*

BEYOND
THE
SURFACE

ALSO BY JESSICA LONG

Unsinkable

The Mermaid with No Tail

A GOLD MEDALIST'S GUIDE
TO FINDING AND LOVING
YOURSELF

BEYOND
the
SURFACE

JESSICA LONG

sounds true
BOULDER, COLORADO

Sounds True
Boulder, CO

Published 2024

Book design by Meredith Jarrett

Printed in Canada

BK06673

Library of Congress Cataloging-in-Publication Data

Names: Long, Jessica, author.
Title: Beyond the surface : a gold medalist's guide to finding and loving yourself /
Jessica Long.
Description: Boulder, CO : Sounds True, 2024. | Includes bibliographical references.
Identifiers: LCCN 2023029405 (print) | LCCN 2023029406
(ebook) | ISBN 9781649630957 (hardback) | ISBN
9781649630964 (ebook)
Subjects: LCSH: Self-actualization (Psychology) | Self-acceptance.
Classification: LCC BF637.S4 L655 2024 (print) | LCC BF637.
S4 (ebook) | DDC 158.1--dc23/eng/20231113
LC record available at https://lccn.loc.gov/2023029405
LC ebook record available at https://lccn.loc.gov/2023029406

FSC
www.fsc.org
MIX
Paper | Supporting
responsible forestry
FSC® C016245

This book is dedicated to anyone who
has ever felt othered. You are not alone.
Your story and your voice matter.

Contents

Introduction

SOME PARENTS ARE introduced to their new baby on a sonogram screen and then meet them in a hospital room after nine months of careful preparation, but some parents—like mine—are introduced to their child through a photograph from an orphanage and travel to meet them for the first time in a foreign country.

The first time my parents ever held me, I was already thirteen months old. "Little Tanya" is what the Russian caretakers at the orphanage called me as they first placed me in my dad's waiting arms. I was kept in a room with rows of cribs, my little blond head peeking through the bars of my cradle at this man who represented a whole new world and family waiting for me. He'd traveled to Irkutsk, Russia, to adopt me and another little boy from the same orphanage while my new mom stayed back in Maryland with their two other children. My dad walked into that drafty old orphanage in the middle of March, locked eyes with me, and didn't see the disability I'd been born with. He saw only his beautiful baby daughter he had come to take home.

When you cannot conceive or carry a baby after previously giving birth, it's called *secondary infertility*. My parents, Steve and Beth Long, had two children and then weren't able to have another. But adoption had been a possibility they'd talked about even before experiencing infertility, so they immediately turned to that alternative—which started my journey through this amazing life.

My mom says that as she held that picture of a little Russian baby girl, she knew right away I was the child God wanted them to adopt. My parents had connected with a team of people who were in the process of starting an adoption agency, and this team had taken the picture of me the last time they visited the orphanage where I was living. My soon-to-be parents stared at that picture as they were told about a little girl in Russia who was born without part of her legs. They knew that many orphans overseas had physical disabilities, and wanting to care for whatever children they could, they checked to make sure their health insurance covered any surgeries and hospital visits that might be necessary. They'd always wanted a big family, so they also decided to bring a second child home from the same orphanage. In December 1992, Steve and Beth made plans to adopt a little boy, Dennis Alekseevich Tumashoff, along with the little girl from the picture, Tatiana Olegovna Kirillova. Our names were changed to Joshua Dennis Long and Jessica Tatiana Long, and we officially became members of the Long family!

Even though he is two years older than I am, Josh was very small for three years old and had recently gotten over dysentery when he was adopted, so we were the same size and looked like little blond-haired twins. Josh was born with a cleft lip and palate, but soon after coming to the United States, he had surgery to repair it.

Doctors told my parents that I had been born with *fibular hemimelia*, which means I was missing my fibula bones and most of the other bones in my lower legs. My tibia bones made a ninety-degree bend a few inches below the knee, and I had tiny feet with three toes on each side that looked like they were attached to the back of my legs. Before bringing me home, my parents considered the idea of a leg-lengthening surgery, but they knew when they saw me in person that I didn't have ankles or enough leg bones to even attempt that. After consulting with multiple doctors, they decided on amputation so that I could be fitted with prosthetic legs and learn to walk.

I was eighteen months old when my little feet were amputated. My parents were able to stay with me while I was sedated. Then the anesthesiologist carried me to the operating room. They remember me looking back at them over the anesthesiologist's shoulder, quietly saying, "Nyet, nyet," the Russian word for "no." It was heartbreaking for them. They watched me as I was carried away for a major surgery and prayed that they'd made the correct decision, knowing it was one that couldn't be undone.

I woke up wearing a plaster cast on each leg with red aluminum poles sticking out the bottoms and attached to plastic feet. Those were my first prosthetic legs. I looked over to see my baby doll lying on the hospital bed next to me. My parents had cut off her legs before my surgery and wrapped her in two casts to help prepare me for this moment and so I wouldn't feel alone in that sterile, white room. Within twenty-four hours of waking up from my amputation surgery, I stood up on that first pair of legs, balancing in the middle of the children's playroom in the hospital. My parents had scheduled an appointment with a physical therapist to help me learn to walk, but they canceled it because I was already tottering around on my prosthetics. My parents quickly learned that I was never one to be slowed down.

Growing up, I remember my parents had a black box that they kept up high in their den office. It was our "Russian box," filled with Joshua's and my Russian passports, birth certificates, and naturalization papers; those first pictures of us; and a necklace from Russia that my parents said I could have when I turned sixteen. The necklace excited me the most; it was a silver egg-shaped pendant with a purple stone in the center. My favorite movie was *Anastasia*, which is about a Russian orphan who is also a long-lost princess, and Anastasia was gifted a necklace by her grandmother that helped them to find each other in the end. I would hold my necklace from my Russian box and imagine that I was a princess, too. I always wanted to stare at the items in that box and sometimes tried to climb up onto the tall bookshelf to go through it myself, which is why they kept the box so high up, where I couldn't get to it and lose anything. It felt like a secret treasure box that could tell me who I was. Even then as such a small child, I found myself questioning who I was and hoped that the simple answer for it could just be found in that one small box.

Every once in a while, my dad would pull it down and go through each item with us on the floor while he laid on his side, propped up on an elbow. "You're part of our family because we chose you," my parents would remind me. We were met with a big surprise three years after the adoption when my mom suddenly got pregnant again with a little girl. We thought it was a one-time miracle until two years later she had another little girl! I became one of six kids: four girls and two boys. I was confused at first about not being from mom's belly, like four of my siblings were, but holding those items from my Russian box helped by giving me tangible evidence that I came from somewhere, too. I was part of two worlds. I'd look through the box with my siblings and wonder about my birth mother—whose name was Natalia, according to my birth certificate—and I'd wonder if she ever thought about me, too.

I always loved my family, but I also felt like the odd one out while growing up. I wasn't treated any differently than my other siblings, yet I was always the different one in my mind because of my legs. And once I understood what adoption was, I realized I was also different because of how I came to my family. Although my brother didn't have a desire to know more about his past, I had so many questions about where I came from and why I was given up. These early realizations about my differences from everyone else around me were the first seeds of a years-long battle within me. A battle to feel worthy of this second chance, at having a new life, of being different. A battle rooted in a fear of abandonment, understanding that I'd already been abandoned once. A fear that I was broken and unlovable. This battle would follow me, waging on inside me for years to come.

You may not be missing any limbs or have a disability. You may not be adopted or an athlete. But I believe we can all identify with having struggled with our sense of value and worth at some point in our lives. So many of us spend years trying to be the people we think our families, friends, coworkers, and society think we should be. If we dress a certain way, then we'll fit in. If we just follow the rules, then we'll be accepted. If we have the right job, then we'll be successful. We spend so much time comparing ourselves to others, folding ourselves into boxes, and feeling ashamed of the very things that are our inherent gifts, that we completely lose sight of how much we have to offer others and the world.

My journey to self-acceptance has been one of the hardest of my life. My biggest difference from those around me was obviously very visible, something I couldn't fully hide. My legs were a source of real shame for me. And as my shame mounted throughout my childhood, I attached myself to wanting to be seen as pretty, strong, and all of the other things that made up who I thought I was. I threw myself into anything I could to try to take attention away from my legs and prove myself. I made everything a race with my siblings that I needed to win. I wanted to wear all the trendy clothes and be one of the popular girls. I immersed myself in gymnastics and learned how to do flips on the trampoline and balance beam. But none of those things fully quieted the battle that was building inside of me, fed by my anxieties and fears about my own unworthiness. It's funny that we often think that distracting ourselves from our feelings will somehow make them magically disappear—that by immersing ourselves in a sport, an instrument, social media, "being the best," or even being the child our parents can rely on, we'll somehow fill that worthiness hole. Like if we can convince everyone around us that we are worthy, maybe we'll start to believe it, too. But that's never the case.

Our worth cannot be placed in external things—our looks, our job, or the approval of others. That will never make us feel truly worthy. I've repeatedly learned this lesson over the years through my own internal struggles and battles that I've fought, even as the limelight was on me. Standing on podiums and winning gold medals couldn't compensate for a lack of self-love.

True self-acceptance lies in embracing every aspect of who you are, including your flaws and imperfections, and recognizing that they're integral parts of your unique identity and humanity. I've seen the impact it makes to embrace who we are and find the power in our differences and what each of us has to offer. Self-acceptance is a process—it certainly doesn't happen overnight—but we can find our way back to ourselves and what we stand for. When we step away from all of the external noise and reclaim who we are and who we want to be in this world, we have no limits. We can be confident in our abilities and trust that we're on the right path.

I've spent my whole life working to accept that I am worthy, I am loved, and I have nothing to prove. I want to share the lessons and tools I've used to help me restore my confidence in who I am and my place in the world to help others who are struggling. If you can see yourself in me, maybe you can also see that you're capable of so much more than what you're giving yourself credit for. I've included some of the practices I've used and still use today. Our journey to self-worth is ongoing. We'll have ups and downs as our lives change and flow. But I believe that having a strong tool kit that you can easily reach for is the key to moving with the water and not against it.

This book is written in two parts. In part 1, we're going to start within. I'll share some key moments in my life that shaped the way I thought about myself and how we can start challenging those mindsets and learn to accept ourselves in the process. In part 2, we'll look outward to the world around us, taking steps to find our purpose and be the change the world needs. By fully accepting ourselves, we create an outward ripple that will inspire others.

I want this book to feel like we're chatting over a cup of coffee at one of the cute, aesthetic coffee shops I love. I want to look into your eyes and share my story and then hear yours. Like a conversation between friends, we'll laugh and get vulnerable and maybe challenge each other. Some of my experiences might bring up similar hard memories and feelings for you, but we're here to support each other. I've got your back! We can do this!

In sharing my journey with you, I hope there's something valuable that you can take from it and apply in your own life. Something that inspires you or makes you look at the world a little differently. Something that gives you a greater compassion for yourself and your own journey.

I'm going to share all the many pieces of me: the good and the bad, the beautiful and the most achingly challenging moments I've faced. I want you to see my daring just as much as my disenchantments, the full journey to who I am. I used to struggle with vulnerability, with anything that made me feel or appear "weak." But I'm ready to share with you now, friend. I'm ready to explore and share my journey to self-acceptance, through my own doubts of self-worth and battles with insecurities. I'm ready to lay it all out there and examine it piece by piece—and I hope you're ready to do the same. No matter what season you find yourself in, you're not alone. Let's take this first step together.

Part I

STARTING WITHIN

Learning to Accept Ourselves

I

The First Ripples of Otherness

I DIDN'T UNDERSTAND why I was different.

I didn't get it. I didn't like it, and as a child, I didn't *want* to be different. Through my formative years, all I wanted to do was blend in. But growing up without legs, I was faced with countless moments where I had to confront the fact that I *was* different. I had the atypical childhood experience of repeated surgeries and a constant sense of insecurity about my place in the world and what my future would hold.

When I looked around me, I saw that my family didn't have to go through the same pain that I went through. The pain of waking up from another surgery. The fear that gripped me as I entered the hospital again, putting on the itchy nightgown, being wheeled into a white room that smelled like rubbing alcohol, surrounded by doctors and nurses in blue. The whole scene was always so upsetting for me. It was terrifying, really, though I tried not to show it.

I was only eighteen months old when I had my amputation surgery after being adopted, so I don't remember it, but what I do remember is feeling a tightness in my chest and a nervousness that overwhelmed me with each surgery after that. The doctors' masks, as they came into the surgical room, made it all the more scary. I could never fully see their faces, these people who would put me to sleep and change my body, even as I knew that they spoke to me nicely. I felt like I was a problem. How many little girls knew how to climb from the hospital bed to the cold surgical table without being prompted? How many knew the flavors of anesthesia (I always chose orange) or that even if you fight it, they will still put the mask over your face and put you to sleep?

As a child, I hated the doctors. Sure, they usually had kind eyes, and my parents made sure I understood that they were helping me with my legs. But I also knew that whenever they put me to sleep, I woke up in pain. I always felt a weight in my chest as I waited for my next surgery, but the disorientation of waking up in a different room and feeling like my legs were on fire was always worse than the weight of that dreaded anticipation. For me, these surgeries came around so quickly. It felt like just when I'd conquered one and fully recovered, I'd have to go back in for another. I would sometimes avoid telling anyone of the physical agony I was in just to avoid going back.

As I grew and got old enough to understand, the frequent surgeries came more into focus for me. Doctors told us that the bones in my legs had developed "bony overgrowth." Every couple of years, I'd need to get a revision surgery to have the bony overgrowths in my legs removed. When my parents first adopted me, they thought I'd need a one-and-done surgery, not several rounds that seemed to go on forever. They weren't expecting more surgeries once my little feet were amputated; yet there we were, back at the hospital, over and over again. My tibias kept growing with my growth spurts, and the doctors had to keep cutting them.

As the years went on, when the doctors told me I could bring a parent back into the surgical area with me for support, I found that I was often doing it more for my parents than I was for myself. I wanted a parent to come back with me just so they got to see what I had to go through. After a few surgeries, I stopped looking to my parents for support or comfort the way I saw other kids in the hospital doing, but I still wanted them to *see* it, to *understand* it. I wanted to show them that I was really strong. If I was strong, then maybe they wouldn't see me as a problem. Maybe people would see that strength instead of my differences. I didn't want pity or for people to treat me differently, so I tried to prove how tough I was instead. I tried to hide the fear.

We would talk about all sorts of different things to get my mind off of the surgery at hand, but I was scared, every time. And it was a waiting game—a waiting game of smells and images that haunted me even when I was at home. Then the time would come for the doctors to do all the surgical prep and mark up my legs yet again. My parents and I learned to be very specific with the doctors about my history of surgeries and what medications worked for me, and to ask a lot of questions. If they left my bone too sharp at the end of my leg, and it wasn't rounded, I'd feel like the sharp point of it might break through my skin as I walked. As a small child still playing with dolls, I was already instructing doctors about my health and well-being.

Physical touch from others became too much for me, mounting with each passing doctor's visit, but I was still too young to understand why. Around four years old, I stopped letting my parents hug or cuddle me, both inside and outside the hospital. I remember my parents trying to touch me before and after surgeries, and that really upset me too much for me to handle and process. When the doctors tried to help me onto the bed, I'd swat them away and refuse their help. I hated those helping hands. So, I would jump onto the cold operating table on my own.

I would think to myself, *You can't cry, you can't be upset*, even when my little heart was beating so fast and my ears were warm from fear. There was a terrible beeping from machines that always bothered my ears and bright fluorescent lights that made the room feel like something out of a movie. Scrubs, masks, and surgical caps. Drainage tubes that got pulled out of my legs in the middle of the night as I was sleeping, feeling as if my skin was being ripped open as blood dripped out of my leg. Inside, I wanted to cry. Outwardly, I was angry—it was like a vibration through my body. I was once so angry after a surgery that they had to sedate me when I started punching at the doctors and nurses. But I couldn't articulate why I was so twisted up inside.

After every surgery, I would get special visits from family members, sometimes bearing gifts. My grandparents would always bring me my favorite strawberry popsicles, which I usually could only have when I visited their house, since they weren't the organic ones my mom would buy. It was the only time I loved the special attention and the one part of the healing process that I enjoyed. But even my favorite popsicles couldn't take away the pain and frustration.

I quickly learned that if I had surgery on both legs at once, I was miserable because I couldn't move around or do anything for myself in that state. However, if I only got one leg done, I could wear one prosthetic and use crutches or use my arms and one good leg to get around the house on my knee. The quickest way across the room though was to somersault across the floor, so my family got used to seeing me flipping around the house. I preferred the independence of being able to move on my own like that, but I still couldn't join my siblings playing outside when I had to rest and recover from surgeries . . . unless I used my small, hot pink wheelchair to roll around on our driveway.

I didn't like using that pink wheelchair; I never liked wheelchairs at all because I fought so hard to walk on my own. The wheelchair felt like weakness; it reminded me of my limitations, even though my parents had been so thoughtful as to get me one in a color they knew I'd like. But from my perspective, people treated me differently when I used my wheelchair than they did when I used my crutches. The wheelchair garnered such a different response—pity, and people looking to help me, to touch me. So I came to like the idea of crutches more, even though when I used crutches, my leg would swell from hanging downward. I could feel all the blood rushing to the bottom of my cast and my stitches, and at night I would have to pay for it, elevating my leg. Anything to avoid needing help and facing my limitations, though. Anything to not have to feel as different as I knew I was from other people, to not have to confront that question of *why*. You can't really hide not having your legs—though, early in life, I did go to great lengths to try. But the hardest thing about being different from everyone else around me was that I didn't understand *why* I was different.

FACING THE DIFFERENCES

For me, that question of *why* was hard to face. It encompassed so much that was difficult for my young mind to fully grasp or articulate. It was a question that I almost felt like I *couldn't* ask. I mean, would there even be an answer? I was also smart enough to know that nothing was going to change, even if I came to understand why this had happened to me. My legs weren't going to grow overnight. Nothing was going to miraculously happen.

When I would wrestle with that question—*why?*—I was really asking for so many answers all wrapped up in that one small word. Why was I put up for adoption, and why did my family choose *me?* Why did I feel like such a burden—not only with being an adopted part of the family but also as an amputee who put my family through so much emotional and financial strain with each surgery and doctor's visit? Why did I feel like half of a person? Why did everyone else get to have legs when I didn't?

It's amazing how much we can notice and carry at such a young age, how strongly we can feel our differences. We can start to see and think that who we are is "other," and that we need to hide key parts of ourselves to be accepted. When you think back to some of your earliest memories as a child, was there something about who you were that felt "different," something that you started to internalize without really realizing it? According to research from the University of Washington's Institute for Learning and Brain Sciences, by the age of five, children have a sense of self-esteem comparable in strength to that of adults.[1] Self-esteem is how we value and perceive ourselves. That means that all of your "whys" growing up, as well as moments where you dealt with fear or shame about being different, impacted your level of self-acceptance earlier than you could have imagined. All of those questions I avoided were ultimately bubbling up to create a picture of how I viewed myself that I would carry for years.

As a very small child, I felt this confusion about my purpose and place in the world, even if I couldn't quite put it into words yet. If I really dug into asking those questions, I remember feeling almost *too* emotional. As a kid, I hadn't found the space within myself to hold and process those feelings yet. I buried them deep down and told myself I couldn't show weakness. The less I showed weakness, the quicker we all moved forward, and I could go be a normal kid like everyone else.

But in those toughest moments—while going through yet another surgery or grappling with these emotions—that question would come up in my mind over and over again. *Why?* No one had a real answer that made anything better. That's what made asking that question so unbearable—the fact that no one had answers that would satisfy me. I was angry that I was given up for adoption, and I was convinced it was because I didn't have legs—because I wasn't whole. I felt so out of control of my life as a child, like no one understood me.

Instead, I was told I was special. I was told I was loved and beautiful and perfect the way I was, and that it was all part of God's plan. But I didn't want to be special; I wanted to be normal. I didn't ask to be adopted; I'd had no say in it, which was difficult to come to terms with, even as I knew my family loved me fiercely and that I loved them back just the same. But the fact that I didn't have a choice in any of this still ate away at me. I frequently wished I could make a bargain with God, asking for legs in return for good behavior.

This was all before I found swimming and discovered a place where I felt like I belonged. While my family said the right things and didn't treat me differently, I was clearly different from the other kids I knew. When most kids grow, they get a new pair of shoes. I had to go through the process of getting a whole new pair of legs. It was hard to get a good fit in my prosthetics for very long because I'd grow, have another surgery, and then everything about the fit would shift. This led to most of my prosthetics being uncomfortable growing up. I'd have to take breaks throughout the day from wearing my legs or they'd start hurting me.

All the while, I craved love; I craved positive attention but didn't believe it when it was shown to me. Everyone told me how strong I was, but affection seemed fake—undeserved—even as I desired it deep down, and I didn't want to be coddled. I liked being tough and determined and independent, even to the point of refusing to cry when I was in pain because I saw that as frailty, vulnerability, a weakness from deep inside of me. One thing I knew was that I was not weak.

And yet, I didn't *feel* strong. Is it strength when you're simply doing what you need to do to survive? I didn't have another option but to be and do what those around me always hailed as "strength." For me, the surgeries and prosthetics and pain were the only path forward; I wasn't given a choice. All I could do was overcome or be defeated, coping the best way I could with what was my normal. I questioned myself: *Is this true strength, or am I just learning to survive my circumstances?* This question was at the core of my need for independence, my dislike for relying on anyone. I always figured out ways to get around on my own and do things for myself. I'd sit and slide down the stairs. I'd pull myself up onto the counter to reach cups and dishes from the kitchen cabinets. Adapting was my normal.

But even as I was forced to learn to adapt from an early age, since before I can even remember, I didn't know how to express these feelings to anyone. At the dinner table, I would throw tantrums, sliding under the table at dinner and screaming at the top of my lungs. My parents had no idea what to do or why I was upset. They didn't realize that my nubs (what I call the ends of my legs below my knees when I don't have my prosthetics on) hanging down over the chair would start hurting or go numb after too long. I would try to put them up on the table, to elevate them, and was always told to put them back down off the table, so the screaming and crying was my own pent-up frustration erupting. I didn't know how to express that my legs hurt and that I needed them elevated. A lot of what my parents thought was defiance was actually pain, fear, confusion, exhaustion, and a lack of understanding how to communicate those feelings as a child. Oftentimes, I didn't even know *what* I was feeling; I just knew that no one else understood. I got to the point where I expected to be uncomfortable. This made me feel a sense of separation from my peers. This thing that I felt made me so different from everyone else also made me feel that I had to prove myself. I decided that I had to be the best at everything.

At that time, I was unaware of how common an emotion this is in those of us who are adopted. When people experience neglect as children, they tend to believe that they deserve that bad treatment, so they're always trying to disprove the bad things that they unconsciously "know" about themselves. They're fighting to feel worthy and good because they can't bear the alternative thoughts that have become rooted in their minds.[2] Throughout my formative years, I felt that I deserved to be abandoned and that I wasn't good enough for my mother to choose me. I thought she must've taken one look at my legs and decided she didn't want me because I was too different. I took on the blame that no one really deserved. My inner drive to be the best, which has shaped so much of my personality, largely stemmed from a desire to be seen as good enough.

Maybe it was that inner drive that destined me to become a competitive swimmer. I used to turn everything into a competition, even if no one else was willing to compete with me. Eating ice cream on a warm summer day? I would be the first one of my siblings to finish. Walking from the car to the house? You'd better believe I would be the first one to get in the door, elbowing a brother or sister out of the way if necessary. Even while using my crutches or wheelchair, I wanted to be the fastest and was proud at how well I could move with them, even if I *didn't* like how people tried to help when I was in the wheelchair. I was always ready to fight, whether that was getting away with something my parents told me not to do, defending a sibling who was being teased (only I was allowed to mess with my siblings), or wrestling the boys next door. I loved to test things. I wanted a challenge, and the more I was told I couldn't do things, the more I wanted to do them. And I needed to win at doing them.

I remember being on vacation with my family when I was eight years old. We were in Ocean City, Maryland, and I was rolling down the boardwalk in my hot pink wheelchair. My family walked behind me, exiting a small store while I led out in front. I didn't want anyone else to push me and preferred to zip around in my wheelchair on my own. I was going pretty fast as I hit a bump, and I went sliding forward out of the chair. My family knew I hated being helped and that I'd be angry if they tried to pick me up. So, much to the surprise of several onlookers, none of them made a move to help me; instead, they waited for me to get myself back into my wheelchair on my own. Strangers started to run over to assist me, and I glared at them as they rushed over. I couldn't keep the anger from showing on my face. I needed to win at everything in life, even if I was the only one who thought or knew that I was winning.

I felt like I was being punished and I didn't know why. *Why was I born without legs?* Aside from the medical talk the doctors explained to us, I wanted to know *why*, on a deeper level, this had happened to me. *Why am I struggling? Why do I have to explain to others why I'm different?* Even as I struggled to understand this sea of emotions churning inside of me, the struggle continued on the outside as well.

My mom homeschooled all six of us kids—Amanda, Steven, Joshua, me, Hannah, and Grace—and I struggled to retain what I learned each day. It was like my brain didn't have any more space for reading and math on top of grappling with being adopted and the weight of knowing I had been abandoned. My brain was trying to process so much as my body was constantly trying to heal and recover physically and emotionally. As many of us do to protect ourselves before we've learned to process and heal, I channeled my frustration and pain into anger. I had a *lot* of anger growing up. Those tears that never came out? They were buried underneath my anger. The anger was my way to cope. My young brain was trying to survive all of this, and school became a hated thing I was not good at. I couldn't read well until I was about twelve years old. While I hated the isolation of being homeschooled, I was also thankful to have the space to learn at my pace, and I was scared I couldn't keep up with my peers academically. I let that disappointment in myself and feelings of being unintelligent fuel my anger, too.

It wasn't enough for *just* me to be angry either. I wanted other people to be mad and miserable *with* me because I wanted them to relate to me. I wanted them to understand at least some part of me. Then I wanted to fight more because no one truly understood. It was an endless cycle: angry, searching for understanding and connection but finding none, and feeling tired of being different all the time. Looking back, I can see now that I was often in a state of survival mode.

FIGHT OR FLIGHT

Survival mode is an adaptive response of the human body to help us cope with danger and stress. With both childhood trauma and adult trauma, your brain and body take on the role of trying to keep you safe. Our bodies are incredible; they adapt to protect us from threats of harm, and survival mode is the body's physiological response to the stressors that we're faced with. When we experience stress, a series of hormonal changes and physiological responses occur in our bodies that allow us to respond by preparing for fight, flight, or freeze.[3] These experiences can reset our "normal" so our brain's natural state becomes being on high alert and expecting to defend itself against similar traumatic events.

In Bessel van der Kolk's book *The Body Keeps the Score: Brain, Mind, and Body in the Healing of Trauma*, he writes, "We have learned that trauma is not just an event that took place sometime in the past; it is also the imprint left by that experience on mind, brain, and body. This imprint has ongoing consequences for how the human organism manages to survive in the present. Trauma results in a fundamental reorganization of the way mind and brain manage perceptions. It changes not only how we think and what we think about, but also our very capacity to think."[4]

Battling constant survivor mode, I struggled to understand that I had no control over any of my earlier experiences. My anger was valid, but it became an issue when it was used to mask my other feelings and avoid processing what I needed to deal with—when anger became my constant companion.

It's scary to realize that so much of what you once believed was your personality is actually your coping mechanism for your trauma. Was I really a difficult and precocious child, or was I just testing the limits out of anger and an inability to communicate my needs and confusion? Did my drive to win that would one day make me a gold medalist really just stem from needing to prove my worth?

I don't believe in "bad" emotions. And I believe that we should honor and feel *all* of our emotions. Anger *is* a valid feeling. The thing about anger is that it usually stems from a place of protection, whether that's protecting others or ourselves. It's a response to pain, embarrassment, exploitation, and other negative feelings. Anger can emerge to protect us when we're not fully healed from things in our past that new situations are now reminding us of. Or maybe we need to ask ourselves if our anger is simply our minds twisting things into self-shaming narratives that are putting us on defense, as I experienced growing up.

It's important for us to look within ourselves for the *causes* of our anger. By understanding the root of these emotions, we can learn how to work through them and control them rather than letting them take over our lives. Maybe your anger stems from something external that can be addressed; or maybe, upon examining the cause, you'll discover that something in your life *does* need to be changed. Maybe there's a boundary that's being crossed. Maybe you have needs that aren't being met. Or maybe you're facing a deep-rooted internal issue, and there's something you need to address on your own. For me, my anger was rooted in fear of abandonment and a feeling of confusion and unworthiness for the new life I'd been given. Because I felt abandoned, I was waiting to be abandoned again. That's why I needed to prove to myself that I could do everything on my own. That's primarily why I needed to be the best and win at everything. I felt I didn't belong and needed to prove my worth and earn people's love. And that protective instinct that rose inside me showcased itself as anger—anger that was also attached to that question *Why?* because there seemed to be no answers no matter where I looked, no matter how hard I tried or who I asked.

We often feel guilty about our anger, but it's there for a reason, and it can be a source of information and power for us. The knowledge that comes from our gut instincts and the emotions we feel in various situations of our lives can help us to understand things about ourselves and about the world around us. It's when we can lean into our anger and start to decipher it that it becomes a source of knowledge that helps us make better decisions. Our anger can help us when it isn't allowed to control us, as I allowed it to do for much of my childhood.

Anger is powerful. It's an authentic and valid emotion that needs to be channeled in a healthy way. We can use our anger, pain, and frustration to *fuel* our determination instead of allowing them to consume and derail us. What was once about survival of experiences in our lives can transform into so much more, but we also need to honor the validity of these feelings and how they've also served us. It has been a hard process for me to learn that it's okay to experience anger or to feel triggered while also learning how not to lose myself to those feelings in the moment.

Fear and shame are great instigators for anger. They're also our greatest enemies. When our thoughts are turned against us in shame—and turned against the world in fear of whatever failure or negative outcome we could face—we hinder our own self-love and our own chances for personal and emotional success. As a child, I didn't yet realize that the fear and shame I was feeling can make people act from a place of lacking, or that a scarcity mindset will always lead us to feel like we don't have enough, like we aren't doing enough—and, ultimately, that we aren't good enough. When you wear anger as a protective mask long enough, it starts to become part of the framework of your personality. Then it takes a lot more work to rewire those neural pathways that habitually send you into a state of anger into healthier ways of thinking. The longer we sit in these negative emotions, the harder it is for us to change them. The longer you allow anger to be your first line of defense, the harder it is to alter the habits you've had for so many years because those habits have now been given time to carve well-worn grooves in your brain. The more you choose a response, the more likely you are to keep repeating that response. As a child, this was a debilitating feeling for me.

I'm still a fighter, and anger comes more naturally to me than most other emotions. But the anger that was once about survival and protection is now something I have the capacity to examine in myself. I slowly started to use my anger to fuel my determination. It started as a determination born of needing to prove myself. But now, that determination comes from knowing who I am and where I came from. I understand myself so much better, and I'm learning to give grace to the little girl who was angry about being different and who didn't believe she was worthy of love. My anger was valid, but my responses to it and the ways I weaponized it against other people were not. Learning to accept and validate those feelings and how they served me, while also holding myself accountable to channeling them into better responses, has been a powerful journey.

I never want to ignore all these parts of me. I am who I am today because of that little girl's journey through this crazy life. I am determined, loving, aggressive, bubbly, loyal, fun, and most definitely a work in progress. I am joyful and positive, and I'm angry sometimes, too. I'm learning to validate and hold space for all those parts of me. I fail at it daily, but I keep trying and keep doing the work. The angry, fearful, and ashamed parts of us are equally as meaningful as all the more palatable parts—and understanding this is beautiful because they all show us so much about ourselves.

The Reframe

Take a few minutes to sit with these questions and answer them honestly. Don't overthink it. Write the first thing that comes to your mind.

What has been your method for moving forward through anger or feelings of unworthiness?

When you don't really have a choice in your circumstances, how do you use that to keep moving forward inch by inch?

EXERCISE: 4:6 BREATHING

Breathe in for four seconds, and then exhale for six seconds.

When I'm dealing with strong feelings that I want to brush aside or push down, I have to consciously lean into them and channel them into healthy outlets. Doing a workout is one of my favorite ways to get out of my head and into my body, but we don't always have time for a full workout whenever different emotions come up. So, another simple but effective practice for me is this deep breathing exercise. Sometimes I go for a walk in nature and picture exhaling all of my emotions out through the very ends of my limbs. Try this the next time those feelings of anger rise up.

2

It's All in Your Mind

OF COURSE, SHE was perfect.

I was four years old when my little sister Hannah was born, and not only did she steal my spot as the baby of the family, she was everything I knew a new baby should be. She was everything I wasn't. This baby had legs, while I had to be fitted with prosthetics and relearn how to balance and walk every time I grew. This baby was sweet and cuddly, while I was feisty and didn't want to be held. I didn't even come from my mom's belly. . . . My dad had to fly to another country and bring me home on an airplane. The whole reason I was adopted was because my parents were told they couldn't have more children after the first two. My sweet parents knew they wanted a bigger family, so they chose Josh and me to complete their family of four at that time. Then my mom got pregnant with Hannah. The *miracle* baby. And to top it all off, she was born on our parents' anniversary. What a gift. After Hannah came baby Grace, giving me a total of five siblings and a completed sense of otherness in a family that I loved dearly but felt I didn't truly belong to.

Over the years, I went back and forth between being best friends with my little sisters and absolutely resenting them for how *good* they were. I could occasionally convince Grace to follow me into mischief, but Hannah was the little rule follower. As my mom homeschooled all six of us, I was constantly confronted with how easily they seemed to follow the rules. Little did I know that one day I'd learn how the label of being the "perfect, happy, miracle baby" actually affected Hannah, putting so much pressure on her to uphold that image. And little did I know how my younger sisters struggled to open up emotionally to others after years of trying to live up to being the "good, easy kids," who were so independent and asked for nothing.

We all have labels placed on us. We all adopt certain roles within our families, often because of or to accommodate those first labels we were given. I was the crazy Russian, feisty and rambunctious. Hannah was the perfect child, the one who could be counted on to follow the rules. Neither label encapsulated who we really are or who we were becoming. Neither family label was meant to harm or confine us, yet this is something many of us carry into adulthood, learning to fill a certain role in our friend groups or society in general, mirroring how we've always been labeled and what we've always tried to live up to or get away from.

How many articles and personality tests have we read that ask us, "Are you the mom friend or the party friend?" categorizing us into certain roles or shoving us into boxes? We're always trying to quantify our personalities and measure how we contribute or relate to a group. I can't tell you how many times I've slipped into "dumb blonde" mode because people think it's charming or it feels expected of me. We all have past experiences, traumas, or expectations in our lives that we're trying not to allow to define who we are. We all want to be more than just one thing, to be seen for the sum of all that we are instead of just one of our characteristics.

THE GIRL WITH NO LEGS

All my life I've been "the girl with no legs." For years, I struggled with how visibly different I was from other people. It made me feel like I needed to prove myself. My parents encouraged me to try every activity and experience under the sun and never put limitations on me, which I'm so grateful for. But I was still aware that it took me extra effort to accomplish everyday things that were simple for other people, like walking up a hill or even just maintaining my balance.

I never let my legs hold me back; instead, I'd find ways to adapt the way I did things if needed. But from a young age, I started to hide my legs when going outside of the house. I went through a phase of wearing long pants and Ugg boots year-round. It probably looked much stranger than it felt . . . it's not like my feet got hot. The Uggs were partially because I need to wear flat shoes, or my weight gets shifted forward and I can't balance. I eventually moved past my Uggs-year-round phase, but showing off my legs took a lot longer for me to get comfortable with. It became a necessity to me to always wear long pants outside of the house and make sure I always had on my "pretty" legs—as I began calling them as a child—when I was out in public. The "pretty" prosthetic legs have fake skin, painted to make them look real, as opposed to the more robotic looking pole or "bone" legs. These "pretty" legs were designed to look real so that, from afar, someone might not even notice that they're prosthetics. I wore them for years, well into my adulthood, until I was ready to show off and take pride in what made me different from others.

I always presented a very tough exterior, but no child wants to be stared at or seen as different all the time. It was easier to hide my legs than to deal with the constant pressure and irritation of being othered—being treated as different, less than, weird, or in need of help—while also being expected to not react angrily to the othering. I quickly got tired of being the bigger person and making excuses for all these people who were openly staring at a child. I didn't know anyone who looked like me at that point in my life. I'd seen a couple people missing an arm or leg, but they always were older and seemed to struggle more with mobility than I did. I wondered if there were other young, active amputees out there.

My world changed completely, jump-starting my journey through these lessons, when I first met someone who looked like me in person. When I found the Paralympics, I was eleven years old, and I had only started swimming a year prior. I first got into swimming because, after doing gymnastics for a few years, my parents were afraid that the sport would damage my knees. I would jump and land on my knees from the balance beam and the uneven bars without my prosthetic legs. I did cartwheels and backflips on my knees. My parents finally sat me down at our kitchen table and gave me an ultimatum: either I could try gymnastics in my prosthetic legs, or they'd help me find another sport. My prosthetics were not as advanced as they are today, so I was balanced on top of them and held in by suction. There was no way I'd be able to double balance on a beam, jump with them on, or do the uneven bars without one flinging across the room. I was disappointed that my gymnast days were over, confined to doing flips on the trampoline we had in our backyard.

My grandmother had heard about a local swim team and knew I loved to swim. I had been swimming in my grandparents' above-ground pool since I was three years old, first with my parents and floaties, and then on my own, beating all my siblings at holding my breath underwater for the longest. My family went to my grandparents' house every week for lunch after church. I would try to eat as fast as I could so I could change into my swimsuit and jump into the pool. I would spend hours pretending I was a mermaid. So swimming seemed like the natural next sport for me to try.

One year after joining the local competitive swim team, my parents were approached at a swim meet and told my times were possibly fast enough for the Paralympic Games. We'd never heard of the Paralympics at that point, so we looked into it. The Paralympic Games are a major international multisport event involving athletes with a range of physical disabilities. In the sport of swimming, the most elite athletes are separated into different classifications, from S1 to S14, depending on their disabilities. (This is so someone with quadriplegia won't compete against a blind swimmer, keeping the competitions fair.) I was excited for a new way to challenge myself, and my parents thought it would be a good experience for me.

I went to my first Paralympic-affiliated meet, the 2003 Swimming Disability Swimming Championships, as an eleven-year-old who loved swimming and especially loved competing. At this time in my life, I still believed that I had to win at *everything* I did in order to prove my worth to the world, and I was at the start of my long battle with obsessing over my appearance above my legs to deflect negative attention from the fact that I didn't *have* legs. I had started to be hypercritical about the rest of my appearance and needed to be liked by everyone in order to feel comfortable in my own skin. I wanted my body to be perfect, even though I was missing half of it. I wanted the rest to be flawless, and I felt like that level of perfection would make up for the rest of me being gone. I couldn't control not having my legs, but I *could* apply my makeup perfectly, whiten my teeth, and highlight my hair. I could dress trendy and make friends easily. I wanted to be popular. I needed to be pretty. Only then did I feel I'd offset my disability from the knees up.

Don't look down, I would think to myself. *Make them look up.*

We see this so often in today's world, even if we don't have a disability: we fake it until we make it. We try to blend in and box ourselves into what we believe will be accepted to avoid any potential rejection. But is that really working? Because I would say that more people are struggling with the comparison game than ever before. We feel the need to constantly do more and be better. I had to learn to change that perspective to understand that I am who I need to be, just the way I am, and this is a lesson that I still have to work toward learning every day. But growing up, I can't even tell you the amount of time I spent focusing on my makeup or being unable to go to sleep without whitening my teeth because I thought, *If you don't have legs, then you can at least have nice teeth.* I wanted to control everything about myself that I *could* control. A lot of us want to feel control over little parts of our lives, especially if we don't have control over a specific bigger area. This, too, was a mindset that I had to learn and fight to let go of.

Yet when I walked onto that pool deck, surrounded by the now-familiar smell of chlorine, I could barely believe what I saw.

Everyone looked like me.

Everyone was different just like me.

Every athlete had some sort of disability. They were young, strong, tough swimmers who were there to compete, just like me. There were people with single- or multiple-limb loss, cerebral palsy, dwarfism, paralysis, and varying degrees of blindness. Everyone was "different," so everyone was the same. *Different* was *normal*. We were connected, and I felt at home surrounded by these other athletes who were like me.

THE START OF A MINDSET SHIFT

I started wearing shorts after that meet, leaving behind my yearslong habit of wearing some combination of pants and Uggs over my "pretty" legs. Meeting people in person who looked like me wrapped me in a renewed sense of affirmation. It's so telling how simply seeing someone like me up close affected my self-image so drastically and so quickly. That's the power of representation, why it's so important for us to be able to see ourselves in those around us—to see people who look like us if we're people who don't fit into the "norm." I suddenly felt less alone than I ever had before. My circumstances hadn't changed, but my mindset had.

The World English Dictionary defines *mindset* as "a habitual or characteristic mental attitude that determines how you will interpret and respond to situations." I like the use of the word *habitual* because it reminds us that old habits can be unlearned and new habits can be formed. Your mindset is your collection of thoughts and beliefs that shape your *thought habits*. And your thought habits affect how you think, what you feel, and what you do. We can train our mindset to be one of positivity, strength, and resilience, once that's the kind of life we decide we want to live.

I've always struggled to relate to friends and family who give up easily because this has never been a luxury that I've been afforded (although there's nothing wrong with letting go and discerning when you need to give in). That's just not in my mindset and never has been, even as I struggled with how the world saw me. This mindset only strengthened once I found the Paralympics. By seeing others who were like me, I felt like I had proof that I *could* do anything I put my mind to. If I ever messed up or failed to meet a goal, it only made me want to do better the next time. Every experience was just a stepping stone to success as I learned to enjoy the challenge of pushing myself, even if it took me some time. The more I believed in myself and visualized it, and the more I saw it happening for others around me, the more I knew for sure that I could achieve what I wanted—not out of needing to be perfect, but knowing I had a community pushing those boundaries alongside me. My mindset became rooted in the determination to do anything I set my mind to.

In moments where I'm in pain walking in my prosthetics, I think to myself, *Okay, get through fifty steps.* Then I restart and count again—*you can push yourself to do another fifty.* If I'm on the streets or shopping or just doing everyday-life things that are so easy for other people, I know that I have to adapt, and having a determined mindset comes into play. I talk to myself and encourage myself—*You can do it, Jess. It's going to be hard, but you've done it before*—especially in my everyday workouts or when I train with Olympic and Paralympic athletes. It's these small shifts in mindset that get me through each day, and that kept me from breaking on my worst days.

I've found that people notice when I view myself positively, carrying myself with confidence, and will reflect that back to me. Instead of getting the looks of disgust or disapproval that I once expected to see, I now see support from those around me. Some of that is I'm now looking for the positive, so I'm seeing more positive responses. But a lot of it is that people will respond to our energy, and they're taking their cues from us when it's a new experience or interaction—as it is for most people when they see me with my prosthetic legs. How we respond to our own experiences and challenges inspires how others respond to us. It's these mindset shifts that can change our entire outlook on life.

I used to go into Starbucks for an iced coffee, struggling with how people stared at me, or the fear that they would. Well into my swimming career, even though I had won gold medals, walked the red carpet, and given speeches in front of thousands of people, the simple act of getting groceries or showing my legs in the summer still made me anxious sometimes. I'd think to myself, *Girl, how can you conquer all these huge things, but another person staring at you makes you insecure?*

But when I'd think about the other young athletes with disabilities who'd changed my view of the world, I realized that I was doing myself a disservice by hiding. It was when I decided to change my narrative that things changed. I decided, *Can't change it, might as well embrace it. It's not going anywhere. You can spend this amount of time hating yourself and trying to perfect yourself, or you can take ownership and take control.*

I started walking into that Starbucks wearing a dress or shorts, and walking in with confidence. If people asked me a question, it was my opportunity to change the narrative. But the way that people perceived my brightness and excitedness told me something about the world and myself. People responded to me positively, chatting me up in the line as I grabbed my coffee, and smiling kindly at me as they held the door for me on my way out. That subtle shift and the impact that I had on them showed me how I get to influence people's perception of me through my attitude and mindset.

Changing my narrative also changed my perspective on how I viewed other people. It made me less bitter. It made me less jaded. I realized that if I look at my differences with shame and resentment, then others view me in the same way. I'm giving them permission to feel sorry for me by feeling sorry for myself. If you constantly feel sorry for yourself, then why should anyone else see you any differently? But if you're truly confident, then people don't know that you might at times see yourself any differently; all they see *is* your confidence. When you change your mindset, you not only shift how you view the world, but you can shift how the world views *you*.

I've always had that power over my mindset, and so do you. You've *always* had the power to change or shift your mindset, to face your insecurities with a positive attitude that inspires others to do the same. Instead of hiding, change the narrative and go shock the world with your response.

Even on my bad days, I try to put on my bone legs. They're the most comfortable for my body, even if they attract more questions from the outside world. When I feel insecure, and I want to make a conscious decision to hide, I often think, *Nope, now that you've had that thought, now you have to wear the bone legs. You must represent yourself as an amputee.* Because the bone legs, to me, symbolize *not* hiding at all.

I know that I'm fortunate to even have the opportunity to blend in with the everyday world if I want to—so many other people with disabilities cannot. But if I'm willing to hide part of who I am, it doesn't help anyone in this world. The same goes for you. The imperfections are what make us so incredibly beautiful and human and real. Hiding and not being our true selves does a disservice to ourselves, our abilities, and our talents. Being our true selves means embracing the way that we are and loving ourselves—all the hard parts, all the ugly parts, all the parts that we think might not be as pretty because they're not as normal in our society.

In a world where most of us are struggling with self-image issues and comparing ourselves to others more than ever before, the first step we can take toward changing our perspective is to see that we're just the way we should be—and that's a great thing. How we respond to our own experiences and challenges inspires how others respond to us.

The Reframe

As you're embarking on this journey toward a healthy self-image and self-acceptance, try to do these two things every day to help shift your mindset into something that will help you rather than hinder you:

1. Look for the positive in every situation, or trust that you'll eventually find the positive—even if you don't see it yet. It's not about avoiding the negatives so much as it's about choosing to dwell on the positives instead.

2. Aspire to have a growth mindset. This mindset believes that our skills and abilities are not set in stone and that we can learn and grow through every experience, setback, or success.

These may sound like simple concepts, but they can be hard to put into practice when you've been conditioned to view yourself negatively or to seek approval by "fitting in," as I once did. I still check in with myself and practice these two things daily to stay in the right mindset, and I know they can help you start to see a shift in your own perspective.

3

Acceptance or Avoidance?

BY THE TIME I was fourteen, I'd signed with Nike. I'd won three gold medals at my first Paralympic Games in Athens, Greece, bursting onto the international scene as a twelve-year-old. I'll never forget my competitor, Keren Leibovitch, saying "The baby that beat me" in an article talking about our race, and how I was mildly offended, thinking, *I am not a baby.*

I quickly discovered that every time I broke a record, I got financial bonuses and was offered brand sponsorships. Despite these amazing achievements, I still struggled with my self-worth. I still mostly held my doubts and fears inside and rarely shared the mounting pressure and confusion I was feeling with my family and friends. My parents would give me access to some of my money, saving the rest for my future use, and while it felt good to earn money at that age and boosted my sense of self-worth and sense of purpose within my family, I still struggled with needing to turn everything into a competition. I still struggled with needing to maintain a sense of perfection about my appearance in order to distract people from what I felt I lacked below.

I started buying expensive makeup and perfumes. I would read all the magazines that a teenage girl could get her hands on, and I wanted to be a model. I'd deck my closets with the trendiest clothing, though I rarely even wore the fashionable clothes I bought because I was afraid of messing them up. Just knowing that they were in my closet allowed me to maintain this sense of perfection. I was constantly playing catchup with the world of "normal" people around me.

When I turned sixteen, it was 2008, and I was hyper-focused on training for my second Paralympic Games in Beijing, China. My dad always talked about Mark Spitz, who'd won seven gold medals at the 1972 Summer Olympics in Munich, each in world-record time. No one had touched his record in 2008 (until later that year when Michael Phelps won eight gold medals in Beijing), and the magnitude of Spitz's level of accomplishment inspired me. *Seven gold medals*, I thought to myself. *I want to do that, too*. I was convinced that at sixteen years old, I'd win all seven of my races, completely sweeping the competition. Seven is the most events you can swim individually; usually there are two team relay events as well, but we don't know who will be selected for them until we're at the competition. I taped the number seven everywhere, printing big sevens out and using home and mailbox address stickers to put them above my bed, on my laptop, next to my mirror, and as my lock screen. That number was everywhere I looked.

In my household, there was always talk about the power of your mind and the power of visualization. As part of my training, I started using visualization techniques to picture each of my races: the feel of the water cupped in my hands as I pulled forward, the way I'd pace myself in a longer swim and then send my last burst of energy into propelling me that last lap toward the wall. And finally, the moment my fingers would hit the underwater sensor that stops the clock. Before competitions, I would close my eyes and literally go through the motions of swimming, visualizing winning first place, picturing myself in the center of the podium as they placed the gold medal around my neck and played my national anthem. I'd tell myself over and over again that I was a champion to hype myself up. It turned out to be a great way to visualize and remind myself of my goals. It was a habit that has continued throughout the rest of my swimming career, and it was the first step to learning to *see* my goals, speak them out loud, and use that self-encouragement as momentum. When you can see it, you can believe it.

WHEN WHAT WE *DO* BECOMES WHO WE ARE

Leading up to the Beijing Games, everyone knew that seven was my goal. I had neighbors making me signs with the number seven on them, and I'd wake up every morning setting my eyes on that seven above my bed. I just felt in my bones that this was within my power, that this was going to happen. The only problem was that my goal was not just something I *wanted* to accomplish; I'd started to tie it into who I was and how I saw myself.

We sometimes get *what we do* confused with *who we are*, and we start to see our value in that. Swimming is a part of who I am, but my level of success started to dictate who I was, too. It became a personal indicator of my sense of purpose and self-worth—the way that I proved my value to myself, my family, the world. I had no room in my mind for failure because failure could only equate to worthlessness. I'd spent four years striving to be this ultimate champion, and now I'd been telling everyone that I was going to win seven gold medals. What happens when the thing you're passionate about becomes your identity? What happens when you can't untangle your self-worth from what you *do* or accomplish?

At the Beijing Games, I swam in the 100-meter freestyle, 100-meter butterfly, 100-meter breaststroke, 100-meter backstroke, 400-meter freestyle, 50-meter freestyle, and the 200-meter individual medley (IM), consisting of 50 meters of each of the four strokes. I won gold in my first two events, and there was no doubt in my mind that this would be my legacy. I was going to do exactly what I said I'd do. Each event has a morning preliminary swim, with multiple heats to narrow the competition down to the top eight swimmers, who will fill the lanes that evening at finals for that same event. The 100-meter breaststroke was up next, but we didn't have more than eight swimmers, so we skipped prelims and went right into finals for that event. Breaststroke has always been my worst stroke because it's mostly about the power in your legs that propels you forward, but I was still the world-record holder at that time. I dove in for my next event, ready to dominate, swimming my heart out. I visualized that number seven even as I focused on my form in the water, reaching for my third gold. I came into the wall, my arms shooting forward from my chest . . . and touched in third place.

The moment I felt my fingers touch, I glanced up at the board that listed the names of each of the competitors in the water along with our final times as each swimmer hit the wall, and I saw that I'd won a bronze medal. Not the gold. Not even the silver. Then I saw my teammate, the competitor whom I admired the most and looked to as my hero in the Paralympics, Erin Popovich, pulling herself out of the water, jumping up and down and celebrating. She had just won the gold medal, and I was proud of her, but the realization that seven was no longer within my reach washed over me.

The disappointment I felt was already crushing as I pulled myself out of the water. *There it went,* I thought. *It's gone.* The feeling of failure that I'd been running from off and on for my entire life, and for my entire swimming career up to that point, had caught up to me and was beginning to overtake me. Even though I had already won two gold medals at Beijing alone, something most athletes would only dream of, I was so crushingly upset with myself. I kept thinking, *This wasn't supposed to happen.* I didn't even want to face my parents or my coaches, already ashamed and upset with myself because I'd let my dream get taken away from me.

While on the surface, it may sound silly or entitled to get upset about not winning at something that you've put your mind to, it's hard to come in third place when it diminishes your own feelings of self-worth and how you view yourself. This moment made me feel worthless on the inside. Losing made me feel devoid of purpose, because even as I still struggled to make sure my appearance on the top half of my body was perfect at this age, swimming—and being the best at it—had also become *everything* to me. It had become this thing that fueled what and who I thought I was. It had become the thing that held my sense of self-worth. Sometimes, we experience more failures and hard lessons in life than we do wins and accolades. So what happens when we start equating winning to our self-worth?

After every race, we walk through the "mix zone" where all the reporters wait to interview us after our swims. I was still reeling from the devastation of seeing my name third on the board, still feeling the slipperiness of the wall on my fingertips from when I'd touched it, when a reporter looked at me and her very first question was, "How does it feel to have failed?"

That question hit me harshly in a moment when I was struggling and needed a minute to process and regroup. But that's exactly how I felt: like a failure. I hadn't done what I'd said I would. Most athletes would've been thrilled to medal and stand on the podium receiving the bronze. But I was devastated. I don't even remember how I answered her question—something vague, as my head was still in the fog of, *You're right; I did fail.* I just remember how that question affirmed for me all of my fears that I *was*, in fact, a failure.

As we made our way to the medal ceremony I could feel the knot in my stomach tighten as I thought about my parents. I hadn't yet seen them, and all I could think about was what they were thinking. What had they thought of me as they'd watched from the crowd, cheering me on until I touched in third place?

Just before we started the medal ceremony, Po, as we affectionately called Erin Popovich, turned to me in line to go up on the third-place pedestal with genuine confusion in her eyes. "You're in the wrong place," she told me, thinking I'd placed second. And I felt a sinking lurch in my stomach as I corrected her, "No, I got third." She sort of winced sweetly, like, *Oh, tough,* embarrassed to have made that mistake. The moment stung all over again.

I went to see my family up behind the stands after the medal ceremony and pulled my mom into a stairwell where I completely broke down. I was sitting on the step, crying, asking her if she was still proud of me. For her, this was such a rare moment; my family didn't often see me get emotional because I'd gotten in the habit of pushing all of my emotions down years before. But that shame was creeping back in, telling me I wasn't good enough and I didn't truly belong, not even in the swimming world. I looked up at her tearfully from my seat on the stairs and asked, "Are you guys proud of me? Do you still love me?"

Those questions shocked her even more than my tears. Of course, in her eyes, I hadn't failed at all. My family always supported my goals, but they were just as proud of my bronze medal as my gold medal, excited for my success no matter how big or small. My mother started crying herself, and all I could manage to say was, "Please stop crying." I sat there next to my mom on the steps of that random stairwell in the Water Cube in Beijing—still not wanting her to touch me—and felt a sense of relief as she said, "Of course, I love you, Jess. We are so proud of you."

I always struggled getting my feelings out, especially any feelings or thoughts about my pain—physical or emotional. My mom used to get frustrated because she'd take me to a doctor's appointment, and I'd suddenly act like I was fine. Or we'd go in for an appointment with my prosthetist, to adjust my prosthetic legs, and I'd express discomfort but couldn't articulate to them where or how it hurt. Even this moment after the bronze was reminiscent of that—I couldn't articulate to her where it hurt, why it hurt, because I couldn't yet admit that I was afraid they'd see me as less valuable, less worthy of being part of the family if I failed in any way.

I still hated the idea of showing vulnerability and admitting what I considered weakness; pain, tears, and showing too many emotions all counted as weakness in my mind at that age. As I avoided this perceived weakness, it cut off my ability to process any of it, which kept me from being able to dissect and put a voice to it. When I found swimming, I found a space to channel all the things I didn't yet know how to express. I could express myself in the water, though I didn't always have a grasp on how to articulate myself to people. It was the first time I ever felt like I was on an even playing field, but failing at winning seven gold medals somehow made even that feel like it was taken away from me. Even the moment in the stairwell, while assuaging my fears in regards to my parents' love for me, didn't make me feel like less of a failure.

I tapped into my training and did my best to put my focus on my next race, trying not to let that bronze medal throw me off for the rest of the competition. I finished out my events over the next few days, going home with four gold, one silver, and one bronze medal, coming in fifth place and not medaling at all in the 50-meter freestyle. I had an incredible Paralympic Games overall, doubling the amount of medals I had taken home four years prior in Athens. But I didn't win seven golds.

DOING THE QUIET INNER WORK

The thing that I was the most passionate about in the world had become my identity, which meant that my sense of self had become completely dependent on how well or how poorly I performed while doing that thing. There are all sorts of ways that this can come into play in our lives. Maybe you attach all of your sense of self and purpose to what you can achieve in school or at your job, or how well you care for your family, for example. But here's the thing: we all have to come to the realization that our worth is inherent and *not* something to be earned by what we do.

There's a difference between feeling simple fulfillment from what you do—hobbies you have, the job you hold, and the community you're a part of—and allowing what you do to become your *identity*. We all want to accomplish our goals in life and succeed in our careers, and that's healthy and worth pursuing—but we must still remember that this aspect of who we are is separate from our inherent *value* and *worth* as a human being. Our value to the world and to ourselves is not in what we achieve. The moment we tie our value or our purpose in life to our accomplishments is the moment when our sense of self becomes unhealthy. Even if you don't ever feel like you reach your full purpose or potential, you're still worthy of love, acceptance, and respect. This has been the hardest lesson for me to accept.

It took me a long time to let go of the idea that my identity was in swimming. I had merged who I was with this one thing, and as that mindset got challenged—as I started to confront my feelings of failure and understand that the medal should not equate to my self-worth—I suddenly didn't know who or what I was anymore. The very idea of my self-worth *not* being tied to swimming actually led to an identity crisis that made it difficult to keep swimming. *If my worth is not in swimming, then why do I keep swimming?* I had to remind myself of why I even got into swimming at the beginning. Over and over again, I'd say to myself, *Jess, you're not just a swimmer. You're a girl who loves this sport.*

Reminding myself that swimming was something that I loved but not something that *gave* me worth removed the pressure of success and put the focus back on loving my sport. I had stopped loving it at that point, after

Beijing. At sixteen years old, it had become a job and an identity, without the same joy in it that I'd had at the beginning. As a little girl, I didn't join a swim team thinking it was my identity. When did that change? When do we start seeing our value only in what we can contribute?

We live in a culture that idolizes striving and is all about productivity. We congratulate each other on overextending ourselves and not getting enough sleep in order to do more and be more. In our society, the more we accomplish and the greater the level of success we achieve in our field equates to our value as human beings. And while my voice did begin to carry more individual weight after I started winning medals, accomplishing something that our society deemed impressive, there's no award for simply working on yourself and maturing internally outside of the public eye. There's no parade for learning how to manage your emotions or be a better partner. So many of us strive for these external accolades that will gain us praise instead of working on our own internal emotional foundations. This is often how we get trapped in the cycle of equating our value and self-worth with our goals, careers, and accolades in the first place. If there is no praise for inner work, then we reach for the praise of what we can contribute to the world and the outer image that this builds around us.

There has been a collective shift in this mindset in the Millennial and Gen Z generations in particular, where we're learning more and more about these areas of trauma and growth earlier in life and starting to take ownership of what healing looks like. With the help of the internet, and especially as we tried to stay sane during the COVID-19 pandemic by connecting online and sharing ways to take care of our mental health, it has become more normal to talk about our struggles. In a world of "Be a man" and "Therapy is for crazy people," we're seeing a generational shift toward digging deeper and understanding our mental health as individuals and as a society. I follow a few Instagram and TikTok accounts specifically geared toward helping people to be more well-rounded humans and break the cycles of trauma they grew up with. We now all have access to more specific language to express these sentiments and more studies geared toward understanding ourselves and how the human mind works.

I really hope this continues. I hope we can appreciate that not all success is flashy and tangible. Sometimes the greatest work we can do is the quietest.

Coming out of the 2008 Paralympic Games in Beijing, I needed to take a step back and start doing that quieter work within myself. I was nervous going into those Games, and I was frustrated and heartbroken coming out. Nervous because of the stakes that now seemed higher, with the ascent of sponsorship and financial opportunities that were now on the line, and heartbroken because I left Beijing not having accomplished what I'd set out to do. Following those Games, I had to start separating what I did from who I was. As a teenager, I still needed so much validation from everyone around me. I didn't know what my value was outside of the water or winning medals.

Swimming had always been my first love—the first thing that felt constant to me. It was the first thing that felt like mine. I had a say in it. I had a choice. That's the tough thing about adoption: Struggling with my sense of identity growing up, adoption was something I was always aware that I did not choose, and that powerlessness over the acceptance of the people who were supposed to love me the most—my parents— was something I carried with me throughout my years growing up. I was fortunate enough to be adopted by a wonderful family, whom I could not imagine my life without, but I always felt this underlying guilt that I was not theirs, and also guilt rooted in survivor's remorse that *I'd* gotten out while so many other orphans remained without families.

I felt the need to prove myself and be good enough, somehow. Swimming became the way I could do that. With swimming, the choice *was* mine. It was here that I realized the harder I worked, the more good things came. I also knew that as a girl with no legs, it was the perfect outlet for me to be able to be a force, to be *fierce*, to prove every single person wrong who'd ever doubted me or would doubt me. In that way, swimming had given me my foundational mentality about myself. It was something that was truly me.

The water was my second home because it was there that I felt free. I could hide underneath the water, yet I was also fully myself there. In the water, my natural talents shone bright, and no one was focused on my legs. A sense of comfort still washes over me when I dive into the cold water and feel every nerve in my body wake up. The juxtaposition of tensing my muscles to propel me through the water while my body elegantly glides across the pool. It's exhausting and rejuvenating. It's painful and healing. It's my place to process. In the water, it is like the weight, the chains, come off. In the water, I take off my legs . . . but I also take off the weight in my heart. Endless lap after lap, listening to the rhythm of my body cutting through the water. Endless time to think. The physical exertion gave me something to channel everything into, and, at that time, the time in my own mind gave me the space to process and work through a lot of what I spent the rest of my time try-ing to avoid. I felt safe in the water. From when I first found swimming at ten years old through my adolescence, whenever I felt intimidated by the world and all I wanted to do was just be like everyone else, it was the perfect place for me to hold my breath, sink underwater, and be like all the other swimmers.

But after the crushing disappointment of my performance in the Beijing Games, and given how that destabilized not only my mood but my sense of self-worth and self-esteem, I realized that I needed a com-plete reframing of how I saw myself. I honestly had no idea how to get there, but I did know I needed to remember how to love my sport again—and how to see the value and purpose in myself, separate from what the water had given me.

THE WEIGHT OF OUR INNER PAIN

It has been an everyday battle, an everyday challenge, to feel secure in who I am and my purpose in the world. Part of this battle has been that in everyday life, I feel the weight of missing my legs in a world that is built for able-bodied people.

As I started my own journey toward self-acceptance after Beijing, I recalled moments in my life that had brought me to that point. I remem-bered driving to a family vacation in Massanutten, Virginia, where we stopped at a McDonald's that had a jungle gym play area inside. My parents would put me in tights or cutoff pants that covered the ends of my nubs to protect my knees from bacteria, so that I could take my prosthetic legs off and move more freely, climbing and playing around like the other kids. Another family showed up, and one little girl was terrified of me, even as other kids didn't mind or thought I was really cool. I was maybe eight years old—before I found swimming as an outlet—and was angry that she was acting scared. She said, "Don't come near me! I don't want to get your disease."

I was so mad. I chased her around the whole jungle gym, without my prosthetic legs, and cornered her at a dead end just to upset her more. Her parents came over to my parents while we were sitting at the table eating ice cream and asked if I'd chased their daughter around in the play area—apparently she was also a tattletale.

I said, "No, I didn't do that."

No one argued with me since I was the little girl with no legs, and they went back to their table. I'm pretty sure my parents suspected that I had absolutely chased the little girl around, not only because they knew *me*, but also because my siblings were being suspiciously quiet. Even when there are so many positive things said about us, we often tend to remember the negative the most profoundly. That memory has been a core memory for me—this random girl who thought she would get my "disease."

Later, when I was twelve or thirteen years old, my family spent a day at Jeepers (similar to a Chuck E. Cheese) for a birthday party. They had this one little dragon roller coaster to ride, and I was standing in line to get on with my cousin Michael. A girl around my age stood in line in front of us with her friends. They turned around and she said simply, "I feel sorry for you."

By this age, I'd become accustomed to the looks of pity and ignorant remarks. I hated them and they hurt, but I'd learned how to handle myself when confronted with these moments. I'd built up more confidence now that swimming and the Paralympics were in my life, now that I knew there were others out there who were like me. I put my hand on my hip, looked her in the eyes, and said, "Don't. I'm a gold medalist."

Through moments like this, I learned that you can't hold onto that resentment for people's lack of understanding what we're living through.

But my journey hasn't just been fraught with the ignorant comments that other people make. So much of the battle has been not allowing my mind to take me to the dark places it sometimes wants to go, and instead focusing on what I could achieve because achievement buried that pain for me. A big step toward self-acceptance was realizing that it's okay for me to acknowledge my own pain. I'd been pushing it down, down, down for so long that I'd become afraid to acknowledge that pain head on. Maybe some of you feel this way, too. I imagine many of you have experienced some kind of pain in your life, and whether you didn't feel safe expressing yourself or it was just easier to ignore, you thought you could outrun it. I got so used to being strong and hiding behind my accomplishments that it became difficult for me to disentangle who I was from what I could achieve and what I could offer other people, my sport, and the world.

The Mayo Clinic published an article in 2021 sharing findings about how our bodies can carry the weight of our stress and emotions. It states, "Stress symptoms can affect your body, your thoughts and feelings, and your behavior. . . . Stress that's not dealt with can contribute to many health problems, such as high blood pressure, heart disease, obesity, and diabetes."[1]

We each have our battles that present as tension we hold in our bodies and can even manifest in other ways. My stress manifested in acid reflux, anxiety attacks, and a weakened immune system that easily picked up infections. My body was carrying the stress of being different and the frustration of being misunderstood, both emotionally and physically, every day. My body carried it in the fear that showing any form of weakness, or asking for help in any way while navigating this world, meant I couldn't keep moving forward if I needed help to do so—and that was scarier to me than anything.

My body was carrying stress from the physical pain of the surgeries and the inevitable recovery periods that would stretch long and painfully in front of me. It carried stress from the pain in the simple tasks that most people find to be menial—like going grocery shopping or walking across uneven ground. I have a limited amount of energy before I'm exhausted. Also, the longer I wear my prosthetic legs, the more chance that I'll start sweating; as my knees and nubs sweat, it feels uncomfortable and can give me a rash. These aspects of my disability are invisible to others, yet they impact my life every day. We all face challenges, both visible and invisible, and it's important to learn to see ourselves and others through this universal lens. We don't know what others are going through, so we each must embrace our *own* story.

Imagine having so much emotional baggage and abandonment trauma from infancy; then add the physical pain and the literal weight of my prosthetics. (They actually weigh similar to a human leg—they're just not being lifted by full leg muscles as a leg typically would be. Instead, my prosthetics are controlled by the inch and a half of bone I have left below my knees—leaving about eight pounds of dead weight being lifted again and again.) Yet, even with all of that, I had never just sat and allowed myself to truly feel what I was feeling. I'd hid behind achievement instead.

What would happen if we allowed ourselves the grace and permission to truly feel our emotions without feeling forced and rushed into covering them up with toxic positivity? In our culture, we encourage each other to always look on the bright side and remain positive, sometimes at the expense of our true emotions that get buried under fake smiles and now have no outlet. It isn't bad to see the good in a situation, and I even encourage you to look for the positives, but that isn't all there is and it certainly isn't all that needs to be acknowledged. Letting yourself experience *everything* you're feeling without judgment, and then choosing to dwell on the positive as you move forward, is a healthy and beneficial response. But forcing positivity at the expense of every other thought and feeling is how you bury emotions that have a way of uncovering themselves later.

I would say if I'd sat down and really thought about all the *weight* and the *stress* of my circumstances and how they'd impacted my life, giving myself permission to let myself just cry it out and say, "Yeah, it's hard. Yeah, this adds stress to my body. Yeah, this world wasn't built for me," that would have done me a *lot* of good in those years. It could do everyone a lot of good to first fully acknowledge and sit with our feelings.

Even now, I have to remind myself to truly feel those negative emotions that come up because they are *valid* emotions.

FINDING HEALING IN GRATITUDE

After learning to speak my goals out loud and use that self-encouragement as momentum, the next step in my journey was acknowledging my own pain that I'd been suppressing. I needed to acknowledge that I had an unhealthy relationship between my sense of self-worth and my value as a swimmer that wouldn't allow me to feel true self-acceptance. We're allowed to feel the weight of our emotions and to acknowledge that our circumstances *can be* really hard. That's okay for us to do. In fact, it's *necessary* for us to do.

Through this, I was able to come to a point of acceptance. I realized that it's only when you accept your circumstances, without being in denial about them or avoiding them, that you can fully utilize those same circumstances as weapons or assets. This is when you can control your emotions within your circumstances so they don't control you. You may not be able to control everything that happens to you, but you can decide to not let it emotionally hinder you.

After Beijing, I would catch myself saying passively negative remarks to myself throughout the day in my mind, both about my body image and about my self-worth. *You're not good enough*, I would think to myself on a near-daily basis. *You just can't do anything right.* I'd get easily upset when I couldn't reach things that were high up or get especially frustrated that switching the shoes on my prosthetics was such an effort. I'd get aggravated or discouraged when I put on my legs, knowing that I was going to be in pain. I felt stupid all the time, whether I was back homeschooling with my siblings between practice and events or just staring at myself in the mirror. The brain is a powerful thing. It believes the negative stuff, but I've found that it also believes the good stuff. Even in the middle of feeling sad or down, I'd start reminding myself that those mean and vicious thoughts weren't true. I started a practice of intentionally speaking positive things to myself, too—*out loud*. When I was feeling really bad about myself, I'd stare in the mirror and exclaim, "No!"

I'd literally say my name out loud: "Jess, stop. You are beautiful in the way that you are created. This is your body. It has done so much for you." This has been instrumental to my finding healing in gratitude.

When we're in the throes of self-doubt and questioning our own self-worth, how often do we just slow down and think about all that our bodies have done for us? My body has gotten me through some of the toughest times, the hardest surgeries, the most difficult moments, and I'm sure it's the same with everyone in one way or another. Even if we have disabilities or outwardly appear different from the people around us, our bodies carry us through each day, regulating themselves and pushing us forward.

I had to confront myself with the question, *Why am I so mean to myself?* My body is amazing, and it has done amazing things, even as it's going to go through different seasons. Even now, as I'm writing this, I'm in a season where I've gained some weight, and that's just the reality. I'm not in intense training right now. I'm traveling and doing speaking engagements, and my routine's a little off-balance. I don't always like the way I look in the mirror, but I've also been in a season where I weighed more than I do now, and I was so confident and felt good about my body. When it's all said and done, it comes down to having a choice. Our thoughts become a choice. Sometimes, we choose to self-abuse with negative thoughts, and those choices eventually become our habits. Overcoming our sense of self-doubt and lack of self-worth is about continuing to find ways to break those bad habits. And practicing feeling and expressing gratitude for yourself is key to breaking those habits. Practicing gratitude drastically changed my life. It's incredible how focusing on the good—no matter how small—can completely change your attitude. And it's easy! Anyone can stop for one minute and think of something good. Maybe you had time for an iced coffee, or woke up on time, or maybe you simply got some fresh air. Taking a moment to focus on the good immediately shifts your outlook into a space of gratitude. And when you bring this practice even deeper and find things to be grateful for about yourself, then it gets really good.

Grace and gratitude are powerful. They're healing when shown toward ourselves, and they build connection and compassion when shown to others. Our inner power grows through giving grace where we spot weakness. Through this process, I have learned over and over again that fluctuating feelings, including those we have about ourselves, are normal and that we must learn to give ourselves grace. In doing so, we learn to choose gratitude and the positive thoughts that align with our goals without avoiding acknowledging the negative feelings that may surface from time to time. Through this, we learn to develop forgiveness for ourselves and for others, and we learn that it can be a process to fully love and accept ourselves; remember, it doesn't always happen overnight. But we must accept ourselves fully so we can live fully.

The Reframe

When you wake up in the morning before you start your day, try this 3-2-1 gratitude exercise I love. Take a deep breath in and out, then look at yourself in the mirror and:

1. Say out loud three specific things you absolutely love about yourself. Don't get stuck on this. Say the first thing that comes to your mind. It could be that you love the color of your eyes, or you love that you're a reader.

2. Then say two things you look forward to that day. Again, keep it simple. If you're looking forward to having an iced coffee, say it!

3. Finally, choose one encouraging or uplifting thing to say to yourself.

It doesn't really matter how many things you choose to list, but this 3-2-1 method can be a good starting place as you get used to incorporating this practice into your daily routine, especially if even just the idea of this practice makes you feel uncomfortable or silly. In fact, if this practice makes you feel uncomfortable or silly, then you should do it *all the more*, until you *don't* feel silly looking into your own eyes and saying how much you appreciate yourself, until you don't feel uncomfortable owning your own self-worth. Maybe you're not someone who's used to talking to yourself, but try this every day for one week, and see if you start to feel a difference. Find a mirror away from anyone who may live in your home, and start appreciating yourself.

You deserve to hear all the same loving things from yourself that you would say to a close friend. You can speak entire lists out loud if you want, or give an entire monologue about every beautiful thing about you, inside and out. You know the way you speak to your best friend when they're down on themselves and need a reminder that they're incredible and loved and full of purpose? Start doing that for yourself.

Another practice that has helped me in the past is to place a picture of my childhood self on a mirror before I start doing my self-affirmations and visualizing my goals for the day. Try this for yourself: Tell that little person in the picture what you have to say about yourself for the day. Would you say mean things to that little, innocent person that you once were? Then why would you say mean things to yourself now?

Words hold a power that will affect you on a deeper level, even if you don't consider yourself to be an "affirmations person." You spend the most time with yourself. Start getting vocal in your mirror and being your own biggest advocate.

4

Two Worlds Collide

COMING OUT OF the Paralympic Games in 2008, I knew I needed a reset. Years of pushing down my pain, pretending I was fine, had finally caught up with me. I was physically exhausted and emotionally depleted, and I knew that if I wanted to show up at the next Games in a healthy way that I needed to stop ignoring all of the pain I felt. So that's exactly what I did. I stopped putting so much pressure on myself and remembered that this all started because I was just a girl who loved to swim. I went into the London Games in 2012 wanting to have fun and revel in the joy of swimming and competing. We train for four years leading up to each Paralympics, with other meets sprinkled throughout the years, and I wasn't going to let myself get distracted or stressed out this time. I visualized my races every morning and spoke words of affirmation to myself whenever I had a mirror to look in. I gave it everything I had, and I finished out the competition happy with one bronze, two silver, and five gold medals. I felt strong and proud of what I'd accomplished. But, of course, life was going to test my progress.

Right before the London Games, I mentioned in an interview that I'd like to search for and meet my birth mother one day. I had questions that only my mother would be able to answer, and I had pictured that moment a thousand times. But "one day" in my mind was always in the distant future. I wasn't at all prepared for what would happen while I was in London.

At the Games, Russian reporters approached me telling me they had located my biological family, and Russian athletes started passing me notes in the Olympic and Paralympic Village. The notes contained phone numbers for me to call, saying they'd found my family in Russia and wanted to arrange for me to meet them. One day, someone followed me back to my building in the Paralympic Village demanding an answer, so the officials with Team USA ended up putting a bodyguard with me the last couple days of competition as these encounters started getting more frequent and aggressive. I was confused and wasn't sure if it was true or some way to try to throw me off my game for competition, so I put these messages out of my mind and tried to focus on my races.

After the Games, I came back to multiple video links that had been sent to me through text and Facebook Messenger, showing my biological family on a popular talk show in Russia. Everything was in Russian, but between Google Translate and a Russian friend of mine from the synchronized swimming team, we were able to translate what was being said. It turned out that my mother had married my father after they put me up for adoption, and then they had three more children together—first, Anastasia, and then the twins, Dasha and Oleg. I had always pictured a mother, fixating solely on her, but I apparently had an entire family over in Russia.

Thanks to social media, I was able to get in touch with my biological mother and sister, Anastasia, over Facebook. Anastasia is the one who first reached out to me, and then she connected me to my mother, Natalia. That first conversation with Anastasia was so sweet. We gave updates on our lives, and she wrote that they loved me and were praying for me. I was sitting on my bed during this first conversation and got choked up as I responded, "I love you, too." It was surreal talking to them while feeling like we lived in completely different worlds. I remember my dad walking by me in that moment while I was messaging Anastasia, and he gave me a smile and asked, "Talking to your sister?" I immediately told him to go away as I felt a rush of embarrassment. It felt private to me. For some reason it didn't feel safe to name—to myself or anyone else—all of the emotions that were coming up for me. This was *my* past and *my* Russian family. It felt like it was only happening to *me*, and I didn't want to think about how anyone else might be affected.

I was still somewhat in shock. I didn't know what to believe or how to handle it. I had spent most of my life wanting this moment to happen. But now that it was here, I felt even more confused. And I somehow felt even angrier and sadder. It was like all of the work I had done was just gone. All of these old feelings I thought I had started processing were creeping back up. So, after getting through the Paralympics in September and then the holidays, I did what I had been doing whenever faced with something challenging or out of my control: I swam. I'd just swim past all of these feelings. I went back out to the Olympic and Paralympic Training Center, where I had lived for the two years leading up to the London Games, and stayed there for another nine months before packing up all my stuff and moving back to Maryland. I joined Bob Bowman's team (which consisted of Michael Phelps, Allison Schmitt, and several other Olympic swimmers) and threw myself into swimming as I tried to process my feelings about my Russian family in the safety of the water.

Lap after lap, muscles burning, I let my brain drift to those thoughts I used to have as a child, all the questions I had as I sat in front of my Russian box and pictured my mom. I used to note the features in my siblings that matched features in our parents' faces and wonder if someone out there had some of my features, too. Reaching the pool wall, I'd flip-turn, pushing off into a tight underwater streamline before breaking the surface, and continue for yet another lap as all of the *why* questions surrounding my adoption came back to the surface.

I've always looked at my life as having all these different chapters and defining moments in it. I knew there'd be a part of my story where I'd meet my birth mother, but I didn't think it would come that soon, and I certainly never thought about siblings, or really even my father. I loved the idea of meeting my birth mother and Anastasia, though I struggled knowing that she was born only a year and a half after me and they'd kept her but not me. Also, my youngest sister, Dasha, has a disability. Hers is an intellectual disability, and they had her several years later, but there was a part of me that felt hurt that they got rid of me but kept her.

I swam and processed, and processed and swam. But I didn't really know *what* to process or *how* to process it. I continued to correspond with my biological mother and sister, translating messages back and forth, mostly having brief conversations about our families and what life looked like for us now. They wanted to meet me, and I didn't know what I felt or what I should feel. I was twenty years old and didn't even know how to go about setting up a meeting if I decided to have one.

At that time, I had some sponsorships and medal money from my performance in London, but that was supposed to go toward buying my first condo and paying my bills. We didn't have the funding for a trip to Russia, but we thought maybe we could convince a sponsor or media organization to fly my biological family to the next Paralympic Games in four years. But, having caught wind of my story, possibly from one of the many Russian news articles about me, NBC approached my agent and told us they wanted to fund the entire trip, including getting us a translator and bodyguard. They wanted to send along a film crew to create a documentary on my journey back to Russia to meet my birth family. I didn't think I'd ever have such an opportunity again and decided to go for it. My dad couldn't take off work, and my mom knew she wouldn't be the emotional support I needed on that journey, so we decided the best option was for my sister, Hannah, to go with me to Russia. I was going to meet my family within what had been a whirlwind fourteen months—from the London Paralympics in September 2012 to traveling to Russia in December 2013.

I had two entire families who loved me and were experiencing their own emotions during that whole time, but thinking about my biological family had always been something that felt like it was just mine, like I was the only one who was going through it. The hours I used to sit in front of the mirror wondering what my mother looked like . . . Staring at my reflection made me feel closer to her as I imagined that we had the same green eyes with a gold ring around the pupil. I wondered why she gave me up, if she remembered my birthday, and if she was ever thinking about me the way I thought about her. But, suddenly, my whole family was seeing pictures of my birth mom and my entire Russian family, and

I wasn't sure how I felt about this intimate part of who I was abruptly being available to everyone.

A ROLLER COASTER OF EMOTIONS

It turns out I wasn't alone in my roller coaster of emotions. Many adopted children grieve the loss of their biological families, their heritage, and their culture to some extent.[1] Even if children are raised in healthy and supportive environments, they still struggle with feelings of fear, anxiety, abandonment, and anger. Adopted children are more likely to experience psychological and behavioral difficulties than nonadopted children.[2] They often experience something called ambiguous loss—a feeling of grief or distress combined with confusion about the lost person or relationship. Even children adopted before their first birthday, who have no memory of their birth mothers, can experience ambiguous loss.[3] It can feel like an ongoing trauma because there is no answer or sense of closure.

But you don't have to be adopted to experience similar feelings to what I had. I was lucky enough to have a loving family, but not everyone has that opportunity. Too many of us have experienced emotional, physical, and even sexual trauma—trauma that runs so deep we don't always know it's still there. I had convinced myself that I could handle my emotions on my own, but then they all started bubbling to the surface when I learned about my Russian family. Every question and fear and that sense of inadequacy came rushing back in. And because I had spent so long constructing a wall to seal in those emotions, I had effectively blocked out the opportunity to process them with the people who loved me. It's hard to look outside of yourself and touch base with the people around you when you haven't yet processed your own feelings.

In *The Language of Emotions* by Karla McLaren, she writes, "Without our emotions, we can't make decisions; we can't decipher our dreams and visions; we can't set proper boundaries or behave skillfully in relationships; we can't identify our hopes or support the hopes of others; and we can't connect to, or even find, our dearest loves."[4] It can be really hard to feel safe in even acknowledging that we have strong emotions, but until we process them, we can't release them. And emotions that are not released don't just disappear. That unprocessed emotional energy either comes back stronger later or is stored in our bodies and can lead to chronic health issues.

One thing I have worked on is expanding my emotional vocabulary so I can name my emotions. Taking a breath and naming our emotions not only helps us to process them, but also reminds us that our emotions don't control us because we are in control of them. I do everything one hundred percent, and my feelings are as intense as my personality. But not everything is anger or fear. Sometimes it's disappointment or distrust. Sometimes I'm protective or unsettled. Naming my feelings helps me to respond appropriately and know which ones need more attention or to be shared with someone I trust.

But twenty-one-year-old Jess was still trying to figure out her own feelings about everything. I was able to express some of the surface feelings that were taking place, but there were deeper layers that I had spent years burying. You can only meet people at the depth at which you've first met yourself.

CONFRONTING MY PAST

Our first stop in Russia was the orphanage where I was adopted. The orphanage had moved into a new building since I'd been there, but I got to meet the woman who'd handed me to my dad when he came for me and Josh. She remembered my father's name and remembered asking him what my name would be. Hannah and I spent the afternoon playing with the children there, who were so excited just to be shown attention and love. They walked right up to us and wanted to be held. It broke my heart, and at the same time something clicked in me about how much my parents loved me. My dad walked into that orphanage and saw me right away as *his daughter*. He got to change my clothes and take me home. He was there for *me*. Being there in person allowed me to believe in the love that my parents had been showing me my whole life. I felt it in a new way as I stood outside of the orphanage and cried. I still rarely cried at that point in my life, especially not in front of people, but there I was crying in front of an NBC crew as I was interviewed outside of the orphanage where I had spent the first year of my life.

We then visited another orphanage in Irkutsk that was specifically for children with disabilities. I saw all these little children with disabilities and knew I had been one of them. I was just like them. I felt connected to my roots in a way I hadn't experienced before and felt a softening in my heart for orphans and anyone who has gone through the adoption process. Like so many orphans and children who felt unwanted, like so many people who struggle with their sense of identity and purpose, adoption and abandonment, I just wanted to be enough and not live life as a victim. I could never let go of or forget that feeling.

At the same time, I again felt a sense of what I now recognize as survivor's guilt. I didn't understand survivor's guilt fully until years later, but even in my younger years, it was a feeling that haunted me, hovering at the periphery of my accomplishments and emotional turmoil. It's a sense of *I got out and those other orphans didn't.*

Countries like Russia are not especially great at taking care of people with disabilities. Nowadays, these individuals aren't as hidden away as they used to be, but orphans with disabilities are still just put into institutions once they turn eighteen, and they don't receive the help they need to live independently. Being a Paralympian, I have quite a few friends who were adopted, several of whom also came from Russia. We understand each other in ways that I'm not sure I can describe to anyone else. Our stories have similarities, but we have our own unique traumas and struggles. Some of my friends have publicly shared their stories of being forced into sex trafficking as children in their orphanages, and some have privately opened up to me about pain and emotions they hadn't yet shared with their adopted families. I often thought about what my life might have looked like if I had been left in Russia. I knew that I could have been sex-trafficked, and I never would've received an amputation surgery or walked in prosthetics if I hadn't been adopted. This just deepened my sense of survivor's guilt, especially as I saw these other little children with disabilities at the orphanage who may never get the same chance that I got.

The morning following the orphanage visits, we were on our way to meet my Russian family. I'd trained for almost two-thirds of my life as a professional athlete; won countless medals, awards, records, and honors; gone through numerous surgeries and recovery periods; and lived my entire life missing the bottom half of my legs. But the hardest thing I ever had to do was confront my past.

Our whole entourage drove from Bratsk to my family's village, surrounded by white, as it snowed on and off throughout our trip. I was more nervous than I have ever felt, constantly reapplying lip gloss and touching my hair. We pulled up to the house that was surrounded by reporters, and the property was blocked by bodyguards sent by the Russian news team that my family had given permission to film our reunion. There were news teams from other stations up on neighbors' rooftops trying to get a visual of the reunion that was about to take place. Our NBC team and translator went first to make sure everything was ready and to plan so the camera operators were not in each other's shots. Hannah and I waited in the van, and I tried to breathe as my heart was pounding in my ears. This was where they lived. I was about to meet my family.

I remember walking through the yard alongside the little purple house, heading around to the back where I was about to meet them. I was gripping my sister's arm so I didn't slip and fall on the ice. I could hear my family crying already from inside the house. We turned the corner at the same time that they came outside, and I was immediately swept into my mother's arms. I said, "Hi," and tears welled up in my eyes as I fought them down. As I embraced her and felt her sobs against my body, there was this feeling in my chest, and I knew that I had forgiven her. She was crying and holding my face, seeing me in person for the first time since she walked away from that orphanage where she left her baby girl, and I remember feeling immense gratitude to this woman who'd given me life. No matter what her story was, she still chose to give me a chance, and I believe I ended up exactly where God wanted me to be. I was meant to be Jessica Long, but meeting my Russian family reminded me that I was also Tatiana, and I am proud of my heritage and my story.

I got to ask her some of my questions and hear more of the story surrounding my birth. She told me that she was young and living with her mother when she got pregnant with me, and they couldn't care for me with my legs. She left me at the orphanage thinking maybe she could come back and get me after a couple years when she could afford to. It was healing knowing she wanted me. I had lunch with my family and got to show them my legs and tell them about my journey and that I had forgiven both my birth parents for the difficult decision they'd had to make. There's one moment I'll never forget: I was standing between my mother and my sister, Anastasia, and we were looking into a mirror together the same way I did all those years growing up. We all had the same green and gold eyes. I knew who I looked like now and where I came from.

All of my life I've been a fighter. It always felt like my hand was in a tight fist, always in a defensive and offensive position. But looking in that mirror and seeing myself, my Russian self, I could feel my grip slowly loosen—and it felt good. I had been working so hard on myself, and part of that was finally deciding to explore my childhood faith. Each of us has that moment where we have to challenge what we were taught and how we grew up and really decide what we choose to believe. Before I went to Russia, I decided I was ready to further explore my relationship with God. In the moment where I decided to submit my life to Jesus, I felt Him start to open my hand up and remind me that not every battle is mine to fight. I started to feel my hand loosen even more throughout that trip back to my past. I still had so much I was carrying, but getting some questions answered solved a lot of what ifs for me. That immediate sense of forgiveness toward my mother and father came from a place of knowing everything God had forgiven me for. How could I not also forgive them?

The timing was perfect, and the journey was healing, but that doesn't mean there wasn't more work to be done. Even watching the finished NBC documentary, *Long Way Home: The Jessica Long Story*, I can see that those tears were not the ones I had been saving up for twenty years. They couldn't possibly encompass all of the emotions and healing that was still in process. They are just what slipped through the cracks. I had gone through physical pain, and it wasn't something that scared me anymore, but the emotional pain *did* scare me. I wanted to push through and ignore it, but as an athlete I also knew that a real injury required doctors, recovery, rest, and work. This emotional wound was deep enough that it couldn't be ignored, and it would need the same kind of healing process that I allowed my body.

We all come to a point in our lives where we have to stop pretending to be okay and start facing our difficult feelings—the ones that we've been trying hard to ignore for so long, maybe because like me, you're not even sure how to process or deal with them. Healing starts with acknowledging where you are in the present and where you want to end up. We can't take steps forward without pinpointing where we are standing and what direction we want to go. You need to identify what feelings you're struggling with and where they came from. The last thing we want to do is reopen up our scars and examine the ensuing pain, but they'll never fully heal unless we acknowledge their presence and stop pretending they don't exist. Forgiveness, gratitude, and healing don't all just happen on their own. True *strength* encompasses being strong enough to own up to your feelings and do the work.

The Reframe

Use the following emotion wheel, or go online and find one that you like. Whichever one you choose, make a copy of it in your journal. The next time an emotion takes hold of you and you can't quite name it, take out your journal and start at the center of the wheel.

Which word most generally describes how you're feeling? Fearful? Disgusted? Angry? Happy? Sad? Surprised? Bad?

The next ring identifies more specific emotions that fall within the first category you chose. If you're feeling sad, is it coming from a sense of loneliness? Or are you feeling hurt or guilty?

From this point, the wheel challenges you to break it down even further, getting to the most specific emotion you may be feeling.

Write down the emotion. Then read it out loud. If you wrote down anything additional with it, say that out loud, too. A great place to start feeling comfortable naming our emotions is to speak them out loud to ourselves.

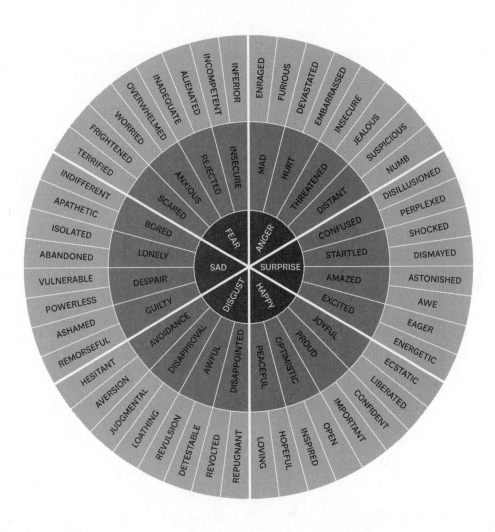

5

Seasons of Disappointment Can Lead to the Greatest Growth

I WISH HEALING came through one single epiphany—just one big moment one day that knocks you off your feet and changes your entire outlook in life. But I've found that healing, forgiveness, growth, and change all take place over the course of our entire lives. There may be some big moments that jump you forward and greatly impact your journey, but they don't erase all the seemingly small moments and quieter changes that were hard fought for.

After meeting my family in Russia, I pushed forward and started training for the next Paralympics, which would take place in Rio de Janeiro, Brazil, in 2016. I felt much lighter due to my newfound relationship with God, as well as the sense of closure and forgiveness I felt in going back to Russia and confronting my past, but I still had feelings I hadn't yet confronted. I'd spent my whole life with questions and anger and repressed feelings, and it didn't all just magically heal with that one trip to meet my birth family.

I started dating a guy I met at a "Flannel Friendsgiving" party my friend invited me to that was hosted by some people from her church. His name was Lucas. He was charming and encouraging, and we started making plans for him to go to Rio to watch me swim at the Paralympics.

It was a whole new season for me, and I was ready for the pressure of competition this time around.

The Paralympic Games had started to gain more national traction and was finally being televised in the United States. Athletes were attracting more sponsorships than they ever had in the past, meaning there was more money to be made. Unfortunately, rumors of *intentional misrepresentation* flared from the start, a form of cheating where an athlete fakes the severity of their disability while being classified, and then swims faster during an actual race, using more limb movement than they initially claimed to have. That would give those athletes a huge advantage because they would then be able to swim against competitors with more severe disabilities than their own. Athletes are divided into classifications from S1 to S10, based on our level of functional disability. S11 to S13 is for athletes with visual impairments, S14 for swimmers with intellectual impairment, and S15 is for people with hearing impairment. Right before competition, a couple of the S9s dropped down a classification . . . right into my S8 category.

At the Rio de Janeiro Games, many of my world records were broken by these other athletes, and it felt like a punch to the gut. That year, the competition was fierce—I swam alongside women who had legs and were *using* them. I had friends on the swim teams of other countries telling me they were so sorry and ashamed of their teammates who were cheating the system. It became pretty obvious to everyone that they were not in the right classification when, three months after the games, these girls moved back up to the classification level they were at before, S9—*after* winning gold in my classification level and breaking multiple records. When there's a gold medal at stake, people find ways to cheat.

Rio changed everything for me. The whole reason I loved the Paralympics was because I was competing against people with my same level of ability—people who were like me, other amputees. That was an amazing experience that I'd never thought I would be afforded. What made Rio so hard was knowing that I was competing against people with a higher classification, when we have classifications for a reason. The politics of it made me bitter, and I was angry because I felt that I didn't have support from Team USA. People were telling me that I was just a sore loser, and I got it from reporters and social media alike. My response, eight years removed from the crushing blow of Beijing, was, "I've lost before. I can lose. I know how that feels. But I refuse to lose to people who are not in their correct classifications." They never took away the records once these swimmers moved back to their proper classifications either. A fellow swimmer from Ireland retired because she was a real S8 and was frustrated. "I can't compete with these S9s," she said. "That's why I'm in the S8 class."

The politics of Rio had stolen the joy of something I'd once loved—a movement that had once had such a groundbreaking purpose, a movement that had once offered me so much hope and pride at seeing others like me compete at the highest level. I left Rio with one gold, three silver, and two bronze medals. I fought hard for that gold, and all the officials on the pool deck left me alone while I just laid by the pool after the race and cried in relief.

Those post-Olympics blues, which so many of us athletes experience, hit me *hard*. I was depressed after Rio in a way that I had never been before. I felt angry, betrayed, confused, depleted, and *unworthy*. I was twenty-four years old, and that word, *unworthy*, still floated around the periphery of my life and of my thoughts.

I have a distinct memory of staring out my bedroom window one morning after Rio, seeing the sun shining and knowing that it was a beautiful day out. Yet, I felt empty and wanted more than anything to just go back to sleep. I laid there for a while before finally deciding that this wasn't me and I needed to get moving. I love mornings, and routine, and getting started on the day. But at that point, after the crushing disappointment of Rio, I didn't want to face the day at all. I had zero interest in doing anything that I usually looked forward to. I had to force myself to get up. I forced myself to get through each day, but there was a fatigue, frustration, and lack of joy that accompanied me.

Even as I continued getting to know Lucas, who later became my husband, I spiraled into an unhealthy place. Needing to feel a sense of control, I started fixating on my body, specifically the desire to be *skinnier.* I grew up in a house where we bought organic foods and snacks, and I'd devour the daily fruit and veggie plates my mom would make for me. We were taught to fuel our bodies well, and especially as an athlete I was always encouraged to eat as much as my body told me I needed. I would eat our off-brand organic cereal out of a big mixing bowl in the morning, along with four eggs, toast, and a banana. I loved food, and I wasn't ashamed of that. I never even considered that that could be something to *be* ashamed about.

Living out at the Olympic and Paralympic Training Center is when that changed. We had access to and would hang out in the cafeteria with all sorts of stations, and the pasta bar was my favorite. I knew I had gained weight but didn't see it as a big deal, until my coach told me I couldn't have ice cream on hot fudge Fridays. Maybe it was a joke, but there's always a little bit of truth in the jokes people choose, and our bodies are not a punchline. Ironically, at my heaviest weight is when I swam my fastest time in the 200 IM. I've never been able to touch that time since.

What really made me lose weight was when I got my tonsils removed. I lost fifteen pounds from the discomfort that eating caused, and everyone started commenting how great I looked and how skinny I looked. It wasn't until those reactions that I thought, *Oh, am I really that big? I look that bad?*

I created a whole Pinterest board and saved images on my phone that promoted toxic messages like, "Nothing tastes as good as being skinny feels," and, "Sweat is fat crying." I started skipping meals sometimes (because I had lost that weight when I couldn't eat after removing my tonsils) or making myself throw up if I felt like I ate too much. My older sister, Amanda, caught me one time and told me throwing up would hurt my esophagus and ruin my teeth. I stopped after that because I didn't want any permanent damage. I tried being vegan for a while, but I wasn't eating enough. I thinned out, and my stomach was the flattest it had ever been, but I didn't menstruate for six months and I felt weak.

While swimming with Bob Bowman's team, we had weigh-ins, which are completely irrelevant to our sport. We were swimming ten workouts in six days, along with weight training. One of the other athletes and I were given an extra 45-minute workout on the elliptical to build our endurance. She jokingly called it our "fat camp" since we were the two heaviest girls on the team, which we doubted was a coincidence. One time I went through three weeks only having coffee and some cubes of cheese (yes, because of *The Devil Wears Prada*) each day, and I'm not sure how I got through all of our workouts with zero energy. After those three weeks, I remember sitting across from my coach, half out of it and completely exhausted while my body had been in starvation mode for who knows how long, and he said to me, "You need to lose more weight."

Those toxic messages can stay with us our entire lives. After Rio, feeling numb and empty, I started fixating on my body again, easily slipping back into disordered eating patterns and hating my body. I couldn't control other people's actions, and I couldn't stop the cheating that took place at the competition I had trained for over the course of four years, but I could control what I did or didn't put into my body.

We all have different seasons, and there's nothing wrong with hitting low points and needing space to heal or regroup for a time, but our bodies still deserve to be taken care of and fed and loved. While I tried to convince myself that I'd be fine soon and that everything would be okay again, I couldn't shake the depression this time. Though I never liked the idea of labeling myself as depressed, there had always been something of a sadness in me, as I battled with loving myself and trying to figure out where I belonged. And when I hit those post-Olympics blues it became even harder this time to feel like I had value or deserved love. I felt useless.

I fought with the idea of depression and was angry that things weren't getting better. I knew people who had struggled with depression, and I never thought any less of them for needing help. But when it came to experiencing it myself, I judged myself so harshly and felt that weakness I'd always been running from overtaking me.

I finally started therapy to continue to work through my past trauma and my healing process. I had never been through therapy at that point in my life, well into my twenties, but this depression was compounded by all the other feelings I had been pushing down for years about my adoption and my self-worth. I needed to work through the feelings that came up after meeting my birth family in Russia. I still needed to work through the weight I'd been carrying in my mind and body for years. I needed further help to release the trauma and pain I had experienced. True healing encompasses every part of you—mind, body, and spirit. I wanted to feel like God took every struggle away when I became a Christian, but that's not how it works. Addressing the spiritual doesn't release you from the work in the physical.

The therapist I ended up with could not have been more perfect for me. I liked her right away, and I remember I sat down for our first official session and talked as fast as I could. It was a big deal for me to show up that first day, and only when I got there did I realize I didn't actually know what to do. I talked quickly, trying to catch her up on my whole story and show her that I was *strong* before sharing the low place I was in at that time. I thought I was there to talk about swimming and my performance in Rio. Those first few sessions, she listened to whatever I felt like I needed to talk about, and then gently moved me in the direction of my childhood whenever I let her get some words in. I started connecting things I had never considered could be related, like pieces of my "personality" actually being trauma responses and ways I had learned to cope. I started learning how to challenge my initial thoughts and reactions to see if they were truly part of who I wanted to be or if they were responses developed in a state of survival. I talked about Russia and my two families and the two worlds I lived in.

A year into therapy, people were noticing a difference, too. Lucas, who had strongly encouraged me to start therapy and was actually the one who connected me with my therapist, noticed I seemed lighter and more clearheaded. I had coaches for the U.S. Paralympics, some who had known me since I was twelve years old, come up to me at the World Championships in 2017 and tell me they'd noticed I seemed healthier and more compassionate toward my teammates, looking to help others instead of just being focused on the competition. I used to hate the idea of the helplessness that feeling like a victim would invoke, but mostly I hated anything that sounded like an excuse. I never allowed myself excuses; I always wanted to focus on succeeding despite my circumstances, and that mentality caused me to be less compassionate than I am now. And people noticed those changes. Now, I know that people have valid traumas and experiences, and we're all working through something, which makes me a more empathetic person.

Looking back, the weight I'd felt was so clearly never about swimming. Of course, I cared about training and my performance, and I had career goals. But that's not what I was so angry about. That's not what made me feel, for so many years, that I had to prove my worth and prove I was lovable.

UNDERSTANDING OUR TRAUMA

In therapy, I learned not only how to process my trauma, but what trauma actually is. Trauma is the emotional response we have to a negative experience. You can't change or erase your past, but you can heal the emotional, spiritual, and psychological harm and trauma that resulted from it. I know I have control over my healing process, and I want to be the best I can be for my future. I want to have a better understanding of who I am.

In the past, I've said things like, "I don't have trauma—that's just my life," "I don't fear rejection," and, "Well, her experience looks worse than mine, so I'm fine." How many times have you diminished your own feelings like this, told yourself that someone had it worse than you so why are you complaining, or told yourself to just suck it up because everyone is suffering? Those feelings were not only discrediting my own feelings and experiences, but also led me to look at others who I saw as having it "easier than me" as weak, invalidating them when I shouldn't have. If I was moving through my battles saying things were *fine*, then anyone who expressed they were having a hard time looked pathetic and dramatic in my eyes. I know that sounds harsh, and I hate that that's how I thought. But when you're pushing trauma down, it has to come out in some way.

I saw my valid traumas and experiences as a reason to fight those labels and push forward, but I now understand that everyone doesn't react that way to trauma. Our experiences can explain our feelings and some of our actions, but we should keep in mind that they still don't remove any consequences or our responsibility for our actions. They can be a reason, but not an excuse—not an excuse to hold yourself back, count yourself out, or, especially, to hurt people around you from your place of pain. I say that as someone who didn't always do a great job with that last part. That has been one of the hardest things for me—coming into an awareness where I recognized the ways that I've hurt people because of my own pain.

There is a balance that we must find between accepting and understanding our trauma experience *without* using it as an excuse for our continued behavior. In fact, I'd say both of those things are connected and a big part of the healing process—we must first accept and understand our *own* trauma; *then* we will understand that it cannot be used to harm others. This allows us to have compassion for ourselves while still pushing to be the very best versions of ourselves. This balance allows us to show empathy toward others while still holding standards for how we deserve to be treated. If we sit in a place of victimhood and never take ownership of our own story, then that's how we continue to perpetuate cycles of trauma and can even pass them down for generations.

This isn't to say that your feelings aren't valid, that your anger isn't valid, or that you weren't a victim. Being able to take a step back and see how your behavior is dictated by the feelings you've kept close around your trauma takes time, and ultimately each of us has to heal at our own pace. You may not have been able to control what happened to you, but when it's the right time for you, you can start to see that you have more power than you think.

You don't have to prove your trauma to anyone, but you *do* have to take responsibility for your healing. And our healing is not always linear. It's like grief: there are different phases and different seasons. You can do all this work on yourself and experience so much growth, and then still have a tough season. But tough seasons don't take away from all the work that you've done, nor do they discredit your growth. Going through a rough patch doesn't mean that therapy or working on yourself has stopped working or that things won't get better again.

The pandemic years were rough for me, even as I was writing this. The Olympic and Paralympic Games were delayed a year, and I felt completely thrown off in every area of life. When I wasn't swimming, I wasn't my best self. I believe there's a direct correlation between exercise and depression, so this inability to be the athlete that I was used to being was one of the hardest things for my mental and emotional state of mind during that time. Yet, all of that didn't take away from the fact that therapy was going really well, and it doesn't mean that *everything* was bad.

There have been setbacks, and I've really struggled, but I also need to remind myself of all my progress and how far I've come. Some seemingly small wins have been the very biggest for me. I've learned to ask for help and allow people to give it. I allow myself to be more vulnerable, both in my daily life and up on stage giving speeches in front of thousands of people. I'm sure if you sat down and took a real moment to think of your tiny wins, you'd have more than you think. Have you allowed yourself to ask for help, even once? Have you been able to notice what fears or emotions are present, even if you only see them after the fact? Or maybe you didn't blow up when you got into a fight with your partner. That's a win!

The ugliest and scariest parts of my story to share are the parts that most people come up to me after speeches and events and tell me they connected with. It has taken years to understand and then share those parts of my story. It has taken years to finally open up my clenched fists and truly let people in.

I realized that part of my healing process required me to speak out against the cheating that had become more prevalent in the Paralympics. I spoke with a reporter and called out people in my sport in an article for *Sports Illustrated*. It was an issue that was bigger than myself, so I had to speak up about it despite the fact that this put everything on the line for me—my sponsorships, including Nike, as well as speaking engagements in Mexico, Switzerland, and across the United States. After my post-Rio article in *Sports Illustrated*, a father reached out to me to thank me for speaking up. "My daughter is fourteen," he told me, "and she doesn't even want to be a part of the Paralympics anymore because it's just so rigged and unfair."

Despite my own feelings of anger and depletion, I knew that I had to be the voice for others who felt like they didn't have one. It's crazy to me how we can feel both empowered and depleted at the same time. I received messages from around the world supporting me for speaking up, particularly when there were some countries that prohibited their athletes from even saying "the C word," classification, at all. And though using my voice to speak up on this issue empowered me, I still battled through my own depression and feelings of *What's the point?*

REACHING A TURNING POINT

I was able to talk through my depression with my therapist and my family, and what I kept coming back to was that I couldn't keep stewing over the past. I needed to forward focus. I also realized that I didn't love my sport anymore, and this was a moment in my life when, again, I considered retiring. So, instead of forcing myself back into training like I always did, I put myself in a position to be around the water while giving back to my community. I needed to find a motivation that didn't tie my value to how many medals I could win.

I started holding swim clinics across the United States with Fitter & Faster, where I'd talk with different swim teams and train them for a day. It was so sweet getting to talk to all these young swimmers who just wanted to soak up everything I was saying. They were there because they enjoyed swimming and being with their friends, and this reminded me of all my memories from back before I was a professional athlete, when I swam to socialize and escape and belong. It reminded me of how I felt *before* I started wrapping my sense of self-worth in my accomplishments.

I decided to take a job coaching a high school girls' team because it got me outside of myself. It took the focus off of me and my internal struggle and put it on giving back to my community. I taught these girls technique, while they taught me to love swimming again. They reminded me that it can be fun, and I enjoyed working with them and mentoring them, even outside of the pool. I was still depressed and felt down for months, but I started to feel a sense of purpose returning to me. I was so frustrated at myself for not being able to let go of my disappointment over Rio, but when I stopped trying to force it, and focused on actively being in the present and giving myself somewhere to be each day, I started to naturally move past it.

Every day, I got further and further into talking through my feelings as they fluctuated. Every day, I moved closer to accepting my low moments, as well as the high ones. I started letting in moments of rest and allowing myself to sleep in some days without judgment. I've always been someone who gives my very best to everything I do, so finding a balance and leaving space for the days I was only able to be half present wasn't easy. Allowing myself grace to not always be one hundred percent, allowing myself the grace to sleep in and heal, was an important step toward separating my worth from my accolades and what I could do.

I started to return to myself while coaching, remembering that my identity doesn't come from external sources. It doesn't come from swimming or being the best. For me, a lot of my journey in remembering this has come from my spiritual belief that my identity is found in Jesus Christ. I've spent a lot of time having that conversation with God as I kept fighting to put my identity in other things. I didn't understand freely given love and belonging. I felt like a fraud much of the time I went to church. The idea of surrender and faith wasn't something that came easily to me. I was used to relying on myself and holding others at arm's length. And I was supposed to let this invisible God in—the same one who decided to make me without legs? I wasn't sure I liked that idea at all.

I had a hard time opening up about my faith and questions. But I've found that there were many people like me who wanted to walk their own path and shared the same struggles and questions I did. The ones who were transparent in their faith journeys and imperfections, yet loved with intention—they were the ones who helped me feel more comfortable and confident in finding my voice.

Now I can look back over my life and see how God has been working throughout all of it, taking me through the right things at the right time so I could learn what lessons I needed. All of my struggles have led me to having this platform to reach others with my story. He gave me my family, placing me in my mom's heart from that very first glimpse of my picture. He led me to swimming. I know now that God can handle my doubts and anger and everything else. And I try to live from a place of peace, understanding that I am loved, even though I'm not always great at remembering this in the moment.

We all must decide for ourselves what we place our identity in. It can't be something tangible because that can be stripped away. It has to come from inside you; that sense of knowing and belonging in your soul can't be dictated by anyone or anything else. My faith is my reminder, but maybe it looks different for you. It could be a deeply held conviction, a sense of responsibility to make this world better, or a desire to be deeply connected with people. I've learned that there has to be something at your foundation to keep you rooted in this truth.

FINDING YOUR *WHY*

After allowing myself this time to heal, I finally decided I wasn't ready to retire from swimming yet. I had been considering it for months, but after my performance in Rio, I didn't want to leave the sport on that note. Sometimes, when something just sticks with you and you can't shake it, it means you need to take a second look at it. Maybe it's to finish sorting through that experience so you can learn something before moving on. Or maybe, just maybe, it's because it's not time to leave it behind yet. I knew the Paralympics were not yet a part of my past. I wanted to be there to compete in Tokyo in 2020. Having that break and getting outside of myself for a while was exactly what I needed before jumping back in the water and starting to train again.

I also started doing more public speaking at schools, with the Girl Scouts, at sponsorship events, and through speeches for different companies and businesses around this time. If you've ever heard me give a speech, you may have heard me mention finding your *why*. Finding your *why* is about finding your inner purpose. Instead of asking yourself, *Why me?* ask, *Why not me?* as a step toward finding that internal motivation.

Who told any of us that we weren't destined, or even deserving, of good things or a good life? I often ask myself, *Why not me to not have legs, to share this story, to live this life that I'm living?*

My *why* went from feeling the need to constantly prove my worth to needing to be the best at everything, and then shifted to giving back to the sport of swimming, which had given so much to me. My *why* finally evolved to becoming an advocate for others and using my platform to give a voice to people who've struggled with any of the things I have. My *why* went from being external, reaching for accolades in order to feel a sense of value, purpose, and self-worth, to internally working on my own emotional handicaps so I could find the strength to invest in my true purpose: continuing to grow as a human being, so I can fight to advocate for others. And in this capacity, I want to keep growing and surpassing even my own expectations of myself.

For me, my sense of purpose came with a responsibility that I carry as an athlete, as a person, and as a potential inspiration to others. And this purpose is now my fuel. I love that idea of turning your pain into purpose—and, in so many ways, this is what I did. We each need to find that thing that makes quitting impossible for us. What is the one thing that stirs up passion and purpose inside you and changes how you live your life?

Your identity has to be based on something internal, and there is probably some overlap in how that influences your *why* and what you feel your purpose is. But your *why* can include other people and the way you want to relate to others and impact the world around you. Maybe your *why* is caring for your family, leaving a better world for future generations, giving back to your community, or wanting to be your very best at the thing you're most passionate about. Passion and purpose go hand in hand. Find your purpose, and that will spark your passion. Find your passion, and that will fuel your purpose. All of our *whys* can and will be different.

Swimming has taught me a lot that has carried over into my life—like resilience, perseverance, and discipline—but the biggest thing it has taught me is that we need other people in order to thrive. Since I was twelve years old, I've had coaches telling me what to do: "Don't breathe here,"

"Move your hand there," "Turn your hip," "Don't drop your stomach," "Tuck your ribs." That constant correction is what continuously made me a better athlete. Imagine if we all had life coaches that did the same thing—people who encouraged us, called us out, noticed the little things going on with us, and instilled consistency and daily processes for us to live by. I've had several stretches of time where I was training on my own without a team, or sometimes even without a coach present, but I was *always* a faster, better, more focused swimmer when I had a coach correcting me and a team pushing me. The same was true when I finally went to therapy; it offered me a small community where I could explore my past traumas and experiences freely.

So many of us want to do life alone because we don't want to bother anyone, or we don't feel like we deserve help. But even if you don't have a life coach or chosen mentor, it's absolutely necessary for each of us to have a team around us, pushing us, comforting us—people to do life with. It's my community who taught me about love, grace, friendship, and joy. Not everyone will understand all the parts of you, but find the people who love and support you anyway. Do the same for them. Depression is isolating, and healing happens in community.

Life is short, and I want to live it fully. My platform was born from my success as a swimmer, but now that I'm here, I know that I have a responsibility to use my name and the opportunities I've been given to continue pushing for inclusivity and reminding disabled athletes, orphans, and anyone who has struggled to belong that they are seen and valued. I'm sure most of us can agree that this voyage through life hasn't been exactly what we expected. Life has a way of interrupting our plans, but we get to decide if we'll use those moments and seasons to propel us forward or allow them to hold us back from our potential altogether. Because you know what? It's still all part of *our* story, part of *your* story—the ups and downs, the failures and wins, and everything in between. We still have so much growth and adventure within us. The battle is not done.

The Reframe

Write down your top five answers to these questions.

1. Who do I want to be?

2. What do I want to achieve?

3. Who do I want to take with me?

4. What can I not live without?

5. What do I want to leave behind?

Finding where these answers overlap or seeing consistency in thought can help you start to define your values and what's important to you. This is a good place to start in finding your *why*—what fuels you to get out of bed each day and be your very best. Now use this information to write a few sentences that act as a mission statement for your life.

6

The Measure of Success

"JESS, THAT WAS so incredibly brave. Look at all you've come through and where you are now. You are strong, bold, impactful, and beautiful. You should be so proud of yourself."

I stare into my bedroom mirror, a tall standing mirror leaned against my wall between my door and my dresser, and speak these words to myself until I start to believe them. I feel the doubts and frustration that I'm so familiar with start to dissipate as I let these words settle around me in the silence. Some days—when I'm feeling unattractive or I'm not being consistent with my training or sleep schedule—they're harder to say than others. I hold myself to a high standard, and even though I've been intentionally practicing speaking positive words to myself, I still have days where I struggle to say them and I feel my mind trying to list out all my faults instead. But I keep staring into the mirror, and I refuse to leave that spot until I start to believe them.

We don't even recognize how our flaws and differences make us so beautiful. We don't understand that our little quirks and habits make us unique. So, we have to remind ourselves, and do it often, until we believe it automatically. When we start to believe these positive words about ourselves, we start to see all of the potential we hold. When we create habits that feed our self-love and self-assuredness, we start living from a space that produces bravery and boldness.

The summer before writing this, I went on a family vacation with my husband and in-laws. Oftentimes, I feel more insecure when I'm around people who aren't necessarily used to how I do things in my everyday life. I love Lucas's family, but I hadn't seen a few of his aunts and cousins in a couple years. I sometimes forget how often I'm surrounded by athletes, Paralympians, amputees, and my own family members until suddenly I'm not around them anymore.

All my in-laws went to the beach that first morning, and as I was getting ready, I was overwhelmed by nerves about wearing my prosthetic legs on the beach. I usually wear my everyday legs, which have skin and look more realistic, but I was going to wear my bone legs to protect my everyday legs from the sand. It was the first time I was ever going to be in bone legs on the beach. Even though I loved wearing those legs and had gotten to a place of being so confident showing them off, suddenly I felt uncomfortable and didn't want to go. Suddenly I felt like little teenage Jess who wanted to wear long pants all year and needed her legs to look real. I remember giving myself a brief pep talk in the mirror, reminding myself of who I am: *Jess, you are so incredibly brave. Look at all you've come through and where you are now. You are strong, bold, impactful, and beautiful. You should be so proud of yourself!* I forced myself to go out despite the nerves. I wasn't going to hide in my room for the whole trip, and I deserved to go have fun on the beach too.

Okay, here we go. You have to be brave. You've worked through these things and you aren't ashamed. You can do this. I walked out feeling incredibly different, uplifted. Even though at first it felt like everyone was staring, I forced myself to stand tall and go join my in-laws and enjoy the afternoon on the beach.

The next day it was easier. I put on my prosthetics and walked out on the beach to set up for the afternoon. As I was sitting on my towel, I looked over to see a woman with one leg coming back up from the water, supported by two of her grandchildren. We had spotted each other, so I decided to go over and say hi. She told me she had lost her leg around Christmas, so she had only been an amputee for about seven months, and this was all new for her. We talked for a little while and her granddaughter told me they were staying next door and had seen me come out on the beach the day prior. Their grandma had remained inside, unsure about going out on the beach as an amputee, so they went back and told her all about seeing me on the beach in my prosthetics. The next day, she came out to the beach for the very first time since her leg was amputated.

I had been so in my head the morning prior, feeling nervous and faking confidence as I went down to greet Lucas's family, but I was unknowingly inspiring this woman and *her* family. I had been giving *myself* a pep talk in my head about being brave and how it's okay to be different, but little did I know that there was a new amputee next door who needed that same pep talk. She came out of her room because she knew she wasn't alone.

We never know whom we're impacting simply by owning our own story—even when you step out nervous, unsure, intimidated, and different. You never know who's watching and learning from your journey. We've all heard that "kindness is contagious," and that's so true. But guess what? Bravery is contagious, too.

If she can do that, then I can do that.

There's a ripple effect when you have the courage to be bold and do the thing that scares you most. You never know whom your moments of bravery will impact.

JUST KEEP STARTING

I've always had the mindset of, "Well, someone has to do it first. Why not me?"

And why not you?

I was recently having a conversation on the phone with a friend, Julia, who has been through a similar process to mine, healing from her adoption and childhood trauma. She's also an amputee, and like me, she's hard on herself in a way that can be emotionally harmful. At one point, I stopped her in the middle of the conversation and just said, "Hey, do you ever pause to think about how far you've come and how well you're doing? I'm so, so proud of you, and I hope you're proud of yourself."

It was a beautiful moment for the both of us as we realized that we don't often look back on our growth. We're similar in personality, so focused and determined in our goals and always pushing to accomplish the next thing. Yet, it was easier for me to look at her life and see her growth than it was to examine my own. It was easier for her to look up to me and acknowledge my wins than see her own triumphs. It's often so much easier for us to look at *other* people's lives and see the good, while focusing on the negatives or the work we have left in *our* lives. We're our own worst critics, but it's okay to be proud of yourself and how far you've come.

It's important to set goals for ourselves and create our own momentum, but I hope you don't forget to pause and reflect, even in the midst of doing this. Reflect on how far you've come and the fact that you're still here and moving forward. There may be a mountain in front of you, but when you take a moment to turn around, you may realize you've already climbed halfway up.

Staying consistent in the small steps we take adds up to exponential growth, but sometimes the hardest part is *starting*. I don't know anyone who has perfected consistency at all times and in all seasons. There's no specific formula for always being motivated, on top of your schedule, and thriving. It's possible to get to that space, and that is our goal, but life is also messy and we're flawed. Sometimes we have to adjust and reprioritize, and that's okay, too. It's okay for us to pause and take stock. It's okay for us to rest, so we can heal. And it's okay for us to reconsider the direction we're going in and reconsider what's most important to us as we're on our journey through life, through finding ourselves, and toward healing. Sometimes we have to start simply by laying the foundation so we can continue to build toward our successes.

Some of the most successful people are those who just *keep starting*. When we make excuses for ourselves, it's often because we're operating from a place of fear that's based in a lack of trust in ourselves. We fear we may look silly or embarrass ourselves starting out. We're scared that things will be too difficult and that we'll give up at some point. We don't want to deal with the shame of people seeing us fail, or with the way we'll view ourselves if we quit. But one way I can help you to *just start* is to clarify and redefine for you what failure and success are.

Failure is inevitable. I know that doesn't sound fun or uplifting, but it's true. Failure is a part of the process of getting to reach what we define as success. It is a stepping stone that shows you where you went wrong, how you can adjust, and how to do better next time. As you've read pieces of my story, you can see how I attached my value to my successes, and that made me much less graceful in my failures. Yet, those were the moments that taught me the most valuable lessons. Success is often our goal, but it's in failing that I learned how to become a better person and a better athlete.

Success is being able to adapt and adjust in every season, always finding a balance. As life shifts, you need to be able to move with it—or it can break you. The seasons of my life look different as I search for and attain balance: seasons of focusing more on swimming, more on my mental health, more on speeches and sponsorships, and more on my marriage. Success may require a different focus in each season of your life. It may look different in each season of your life. But no one else gets to decide what success looks like for you in this season—only you do.

There's a limit to how much you can truly excel in one area of your life if the rest of your life is off balance. When I'm mentally exhausted, I struggle in my training. When I'm not consistent with my training, I feel more emotionally negative and restless. Each area impacts the others. Each area needs its own attention if you want to be your very best. Sometimes we need to reprioritize what we focus on, reprioritize what needs to be at the top of our list of focus points over others. It's okay to have different needs in different seasons. There's a balance to healthy living.

I want to be one of the best swimmers in the world and excel in my career, and I *also* want to be a kind and generous human who's happy and confident. Those things take work, focus, intention, practice, perseverance, failure, and *starting* over and over again when those failures occur. You don't have to play perfect or wait until you're perfect to start. If you do, you'll never start; you'll always have a reason to wait to begin your journey. Start right where you are now and build from there. So, let's take a moment to be honest with ourselves about what we're afraid of and what excuses we're making, and then let's decide to start anyway.

IGNITING YOUR MOTIVATION

Standing in the mirror and reminding myself of who I am in times of stress or overwhelm helps me through hard emotional times, and maintaining a practice of always writing down my goals makes them feel all the more tangible to me. Writing down our goals and seeing them every single day brings them to life and keeps them at the forefront of our minds. When I've fully decided to dedicate myself to a goal, seeing reminders of it all around me helps keep me motivated and on track.

I had a friend from the Danish Olympic team stay with me for a few weeks, and she decided to cut out certain foods—processed sugar, milk, gluten—for fourteen days while training to see what made her body feel its best. She put fourteen pieces of paper on the wall, counting down, and every single day she would pull down one piece to visually represent her progress and how many days were left. Feel free to come up with more environmentally friendly options if that suits you better, like setting your goals as your phone and laptop background, or hanging a dry-erase board in your home, but the point is that our brains like to see our progress. If you want to succeed, you need daily reminders to keep you on track.

On top of the visual reminder, there's also a biological process happening in your brain called *encoding*. That's where the things we perceive travel to our brain's hippocampus and get analyzed before they either get stored in our long-term memory or are discarded. Writing improves that encoding process. It helps with the process of rewiring your brain and forming habits. In other words, when you write things down, they have a much greater chance of being remembered and implemented into your life.

Some people are better at self-motivation than others, but no matter who you are, there will be days where self-motivation is a struggle. This is why it's always great to have an accountability partner to help encourage you along your journey toward your goals. I've mentioned how I do better swimming with a team to challenge me, and that goes for every area of my life. It motivates me to have others around me pushing me and encouraging me. That sparks the drive for self-motivation within me. Who in your life pushes you to be better and helps keep you on track? Consider whether that person would be a great accountability partner for the goals you're reaching for now.

Having an accountability partner can feel awkward if you've never had one, but think of it as someone moving in the same direction as you. Who do you share your dreams and goals with, knowing they're in your corner and will encourage you every step of the way? Who's willing to help you out when you need it so you can stay consistent? That's your accountability partner or your team. Let them know it, and encourage them to keep encouraging you. Encourage them to give you the kind of tough or gentle love you need in order to self-ignite your motivation to overcome your fears or reach your goals. It's the consistency that's our goal here. Your consistent choices become habits that build who you are, and accountability supports us in that. Once you've developed a habit of consistency, it gets easier to stay in that rhythm and keep going; it gives you momentum to achieve what you're aiming for. Those habits start to change your whole life.

As we're reaching toward our emotional or physical goals, we often weigh the risks and sacrifices of starting something new or making a change, versus the reward of success and what we'll get out of it. But this isn't the way we should go about it. There's sacrifice in everything, and you can weigh the risk versus reward for every decision you make— whether you're making a decision about having kids, getting back into shape, getting out of debt, or saving for a house. Any goal you come up with will take time, consistency, and sacrifice. So, stop weighing the risks of that necessary time, consistency, and sacrifice. That just allows you to build up more excuses. Instead, *just go for it*.

THE RISK OF NEVER STARTING

As you're weighing up the risks you'll have to take and the sacrifices you'll have to make if you decide to start on a new path in life, this just builds up your own fear to start, and you forget about the risk attached to *never starting at all*. What if you always make excuses and take yourself out of the equation without even trying? Life is going to go by fast, so you should be prepared to risk it all. I've always loved this quote by Erma Bombeck: "When I stand before God at the end of my life, I would hope that I would not have a single bit of talent left, and could say, 'I used everything you gave me.'"[1] Let's not forget to weigh the cost of never maximizing your life or becoming who you want to be. That cost is often heavier than what we fear we'd lose by starting toward our goals.

The people who are the most successful, or have had true success in any realm of their lives, got there because they took risks. There was failure, too, but they allowed their failures to fuel them. I never want to be that person who sits around talking about the "good old days," all hung up on the past instead of living the life I dreamed for myself. I don't want to live with the constant "what if" of not fully pursuing what I'm passionate about or feeling like I didn't reach my full potential. That is the greater risk in life that I'm unwilling to take. I hope you are, too. I know you are, too.

Ultimately, ask yourself, *How do I prepare for the moments that are going to be hard in life?* I want to always be the person who gets behind the starting block before a swim race and knows that I did everything in my power to prepare for that moment—that I was consistent with my goals and training and ready to give it my all. I don't want to have any regrets in my life, and I know you don't want to live with regrets either. What we often regret is our own excuses, our own unwillingness not to go for what we want. There'll always be hard moments in life, but we prepare for them by being grounded in our own sense of self, our own sense of self-worth, and our own confidence in the journey that we're on.

We seem to get more resistant to risk the older we get. Children are fearless. Their world is centered around them and whatever they want in that moment. They don't think about the risks; they just go for it. As we get older, we start to learn how to protect ourselves and to survive independently in this world. Even at thirty-one years old, I can see how much more nervous I am about trying new things or traveling to new places than I used to be. I didn't think this way as a kid, or when I first traveled without my family at twelve years old—or even as an eighteen-year-old as I embarked on adulthood. We learn, as we age, about the world and about our own limitations. This is all useful information meant to help us survive, but when we start to focus so much on the negatives and what we *can't* do or what could go wrong, rather than what we *can* do and what *won't* go wrong, then we slowly start to check out of fully living. We regress into ourselves, allowing our fears to take over.

I don't want to do less and less and fear more and more as I get older. I want to become bolder and give of myself more confidently as I age. I want to use the wisdom I've collected over the years to challenge my own patterns, to try something new, and to trust that as long as I'm breathing I have a purpose. None of us age out of purpose. No matter how old you are or what season you're in, you have something to give to this world and the people around you.

CREATING YOUR PERSONAL ROAD MAP TO YOUR DREAMS

So, how do we build momentum and create achievable goals that lead to success? I achieved initial success as an angry and determined twelve-year-old who knew exactly what she wanted and was willing to fight for it. But staying on top and competing in the last five Paralympic Games and countless other swim meets, winning gold medals and breaking world records, took intentional training and an understanding of my specific goals.

I start by visualizing exactly what I want—the big things, the goals that seem crazy, like when I had sevens plastered all over my room leading up to the Beijing Games. I see myself on top of the podium at the medal ceremony, the champion in the center. I see myself on a platform speaking to thousands of people about their purpose in life and the beauty in our differences. I have a list of big sponsorships I'd like to get and companies I want to work with. Toyota was one of those companies, and I'm now working with them. I've always wanted to model and have had the opportunity to be part of Ralph Lauren, Nike, and Arena campaigns, as well as being featured in magazines like *Elle* (where I was the first Paralympic athlete to be on the cover), *Teen Vogue*, and *Sports*

Illustrated. I've spent years advocating for the Paralympics and had the privilege of being the first amputee or Paralympic athlete sponsored by many of the brands I work with. So, go bold. Envision the *biggest* goals for yourself without holding back. If you can't even picture it, then it won't happen. Write it down, the full dream, without censoring yourself or telling yourself, *That could never happen.*

Then start breaking that big idea you've written down into individual, step-by-step goals, working backward. Now that you see the full goal in your sights, what do you need to do in order to achieve it? Instead of thinking, *What do I need to do next to get to where I want to go?* which can overwhelm or confuse you if you haven't already envisioned exactly where you're trying to go, you can instead think, *Now that I see where I want to go, what steps will get me there?*

It's hard to get to where we're going if we can't even envision where that is, so breaking steps down until you have your specific, bite-size goals will keep you more focused and driven as you strive forward. You can break these steps into month-by-month, week-by-week, or even day-by-day goals, depending on what you're trying to achieve and how your mind works best. And remember to keep it simple. The simpler the steps, the easier they'll be to achieve. You'll start seeing momentum, and that will keep you motivated.

I like to start with my goal for today and work forward from there, once I can envision the big picture that I'm working toward. Working forward starts with what you're capable of *right now* and builds on it until you have a timeline that doesn't rush you or stress you out. I plan my schedule for the week, building small things into my routine to achieve a monthly goal. For example, one month I worked on getting up earlier. I started scheduling meetings and events in the morning, which forced me to get up earlier than I typically would have. I feel my best when I wake up at 6 a.m., go swim, and then eat breakfast and take a nap afterward. But I realized that I'd gotten out of that routine, so I built that back into my life as I started training for the Paralympic Games in Paris in 2024. If that's something you're interested in, you can set your goal for getting up earlier even one day a week to start. Then build up.

Then decide what your goal for the *year* is. Now that your bite-size goals and new everyday practices are becoming a habit for you, what goals can you add on for the next year that get you closer to the dream? What does that look like in three years? Five years?

Don't be intimidated as the goal gets bigger. Don't let it start to seem unachievable in your mind. Remember, your only focus for today is *today's* small goal. Use it as a guide to keep you focused and on track. Then take the next step, then a larger step, and so on. Writing out your goals takes a desire that's stuck in your head and brings it into your physical world. It makes it real, and it's a huge step toward living the life you envision for yourself. So, take time to celebrate that!

These written goals can be adjusted every couple of months, or at the end of each year, as you figure out what works best for you. If you need to adjust your goals, don't let that discourage you or stop you from writing them down. There will be setbacks at times, and that's okay. We can't let setbacks ruin our whole day or whole week. Don't let a simple setback ruin the entire goal you have in your mind.

In swimming, the first practice after a break is fun and feels good. But day two, my muscles are sore. Day three, I feel tired and have to tough it out mentally. It takes time to adjust. It takes time to create rhythms and build habits. Responding well to small setbacks, not letting them throw you off completely, is what trains you for the bigger things.

This is where my tough love comes in. If you can spend hours on TikTok but can't do ten minutes of ab workouts a day to reach your fitness goal, and be consistent with those ten minutes, then you don't want it badly enough. I'm speaking to myself here. I'm not suggesting you necessarily should be doing ten-minute ab workouts, but for me, this is how I need to talk to myself to stay motivated. I have to be honest about the habits I've set up for myself and what I need to change. I have to decide how badly I want it.

The good news is that once our goals become a habit for us, it's easier to get back into it after you've had a setback or fallen out of your routine. I've been training for so long that even when I'm coming back after a surgery or shoulder injury and I'm not in my best shape, I can still jump in the water and swim well. I have a solid foundation laid that makes it easier on me when I'm struggling through my day or struggling toward my next goal. Pushing yourself to *just start* and then *be consistent* in these smaller goals is important, because it lays the foundation for when you're handling the bigger goals and setbacks later on.

It's about showing up, even when you're not feeling motivated. It's about working through the mental blocks. It's about reaching out to talk to a trusted friend when you need to, so that you don't get trapped in your head in negative thought patterns. And it's about adjusting when needed, which for me can look like, "I don't have the energy for a full two-hour swim practice after traveling all weekend, so I'll do an easier forty-five minute set and then some weights at the house." It's about creating small habits that build your consistency muscles. Your capacity expands to get you through the tougher times once you've handled adversity in the past and learned how to respond to it. You've built character in that way, and you've worked those muscles already.

KEEP DOING THE WORK

I've had so many seasons where I didn't want to show up, where I was down on my body or focused on what I lacked. I have to remind myself of everything that my body has done for me and continues to do. It's so easy to take your feelings of inadequacy inward and feel bad about yourself, but taking control and loving yourself enough to make the changes you want is inspiring. I feel my best when I'm working out and using my body. I love seeing other people at the gym. I hope it makes them feel as empowered as it makes me feel. I get emotional when I see people just starting out on their journey, because I know what it takes to get out there and start. Sure, there's a natural release of endorphins and dopamine we experience as we exercise, but I'm also reminded of how much I'm capable of as I'm sweating and feeling my muscles work through each set. Even in my weakest or most self-judgmental moments, my body is still powerful and capable.

I'm also inspired by my friends who are in therapy and actively addressing growth in emotional areas. Physical, mental, and emotional health all go hand in hand. We must care for every part of ourselves. We do all of these practices and the internal work for ourselves so we can show up fully and at our best to every season and circumstance. But we also do it to make a positive impact and inspire others to be the best version of themselves.

Life is hard and we have a lot left to do. But you're here, putting in the work to become the very best and healthiest version of you. You're living and breathing and moving forward. Look at how far you've come, pushing through every hard day and tough moment. You did that. You have the power to do so much. You're strong, bold, impactful, and beautiful. You should be so proud of yourself.

The Reframe

Consistency in the small things is the only way to also be consistent in the bigger things. We have to build our consistency muscles.

What is one small change you can make each day toward growth? Take a moment to think about it.

Maybe that just looks like focusing 15 minutes on something that is good for your soul but usually gets pushed aside, like reading a book or going for a walk. Choose one thing you'd like to focus on for a week. Start small. Maybe it's drinking one more glass of water a day. Notice how you feel after you've done that thing every day for one week.

Part 2

BEYOND OURSELVES

Creating Change in the World Around Us

7

Trusting Your Voice

I'M ALWAYS VERY sure about what I want, and I've realized that not everyone is like this. Some people have a more laissez-faire attitude about life and are easygoing, while some people care about the direction their life is taking but aren't sure how to express what they want to themselves or to the outside world. Sometimes we may not be able to express what we want because we're worried about upsetting someone, or we just aren't in touch with ourselves enough to know specifically what our own needs are. I'm the person who will request a different table at a restaurant, choose where we're going when a group can't decide, and always ask questions. My mentality is *Why not ask for what you want?*

If someone else wants something that contradicts what I've requested, then that creates the opportunity for healthy dialogue and compromise. I've seen that as long as you're nice about it, people rarely mind and will usually accommodate you—so why not ask?

Treating people with kindness and respect, coupled with the ability to express exactly what you desire, are skills that will take you far. The problem is, many people only do one or the other—*either* we always express what we want *or* we're always more focused on accommodating other people, to the point that stating our needs and desires seems "selfish" or disrespectful to some people these days. The result is that we've developed a culture of Karens and codependents.

Codependency is when a person caters to the needs of someone else to the point of abandoning their *own* needs and beliefs. They lose sight of themselves as they're trying to people-please and be a "nice" person all the time. There's a part of each one of us that wants to control people's perceptions of us. We want those around us, especially those we truly care about, to see us as good or right. While we all seek acceptance and connection, people-pleasing is still just another way that people try to control those around them. It's trying to manipulate a certain response out of an individual or group and get them to feel a specific way toward you, to the extreme that sometimes you end up angry at them when they don't end up acting or feeling the way you think they should. A people-pleaser may think, *I worked so hard doing all of these kind things and overwhelming myself, but that person still commented on the one thing I did wrong*, and then develop an inner sensitivity or animosity toward that person without ever addressing it because they still don't want to cause any waves.

This is an extreme that I think more of us fall into than we'd care to admit. It initially appears easier to say yes to everyone and win affection by doing what everyone else wants. But you can only abandon yourself for so long before bitterness starts taking root and subtly destroying relationships. Ultimately, we can't control people around us, even if we are doing it as a means to create a safe environment for ourselves.

To the opposite extreme, you're probably familiar with the term *Karen*. It's a pejorative term used as slang, typically for a white woman who is perceived as entitled or demanding beyond the scope of what's normal. Karens usually state their needs and opinions, but with a level of disrespect and lack of compassion for others. I think the root cause of people lacking a sense of empathy and kindness stems from entitlement or anger. This name has turned into an umbrella term describing anyone who comes across this way.

This response is still a way of controlling those around us, trying to force the outcome we want, disregarding or hurting others in the process. Instead of living on either unhealthy side of this line, putting our energy into forcing other people to respond how we want, we should instead take the more balanced approach of advocating for ourselves while also educating ourselves—and advocating for each other while also educating each other.

TIME'S UP

We live in the information age and have access to all the knowledge in the world at our fingertips. There's no need for us to cater to chosen ignorance any longer. One part of me wants to be respectful and kind, but another part of me wants to hit you with some tough love and say, "Time's up! We have the internet. We have so many resources from which to learn about each other, so learn about disabilities and people who are different from you. Don't *choose* ignorance."

There's a time and place for everything, and the time and place to shift our mindsets toward a more emotionally healthy viewpoint on the world around us and our place within it is here and now. We all have an individual responsibility to use the information available to us to educate ourselves. We can't know everything about everyone, so of course there is always room for grace, but the effort needs to be there. There's a difference between not knowing something because you haven't been exposed to it and not knowing something because you're actively refusing to learn about it.

I go through much of my life educating people in small ways on disabilities. Daily comments and interactions about my legs are the norm for me—whether the comments are hurtful or complimentary. I usually don't mind such comments when I know someone means well or is just trying to be kind, but I've also dealt with a lot of ignorance, even people who think I'm lying about being disabled. People seem to assume I'm not disabled just because I'm young and walking. It's hard for me to not get an attitude with them or to assume someone is about to be mean to me when they walk up to me as I'm parking my car in a handicapped spot, for example, or traveling in the airport. Too many times I've had to deal with rudeness regarding something I live with every day. Sometimes I walk with an exaggerated limp when I get into the handicapped line at the airport just to avoid people saying anything to me. It used to not be as bad, but people have gotten bolder in their comments and the looks they send me.

What hurts the most is knowing so many young amputees who are experiencing the same things. It's nice to talk with friends and know

I'm not alone in my experience, but it also really sucks to know they're experiencing this stuff, too. Yet, as we're on our journey to and beyond self-acceptance, emotional health, and positive understanding about ourselves, it's important to also recognize that there will be times that we'll *need* to speak up for ourselves in order to *protect* our sense of self-worth, emotional safety, and well-being. There will be times that we have to speak up to the angry and entitled and to those who choose ignorance over understanding.

I once had a dehumanizing experience at the Tampa airport that tested my confidence and willingness to speak up. I was stopped and pulled to the side by the TSA, which is normal for me because of my prosthetics, but the TSA agent looked so uncomfortable and unsure about it this time. I told her the airport protocol is that they usually swab my knee, ankle, and shoe, but after a few seconds she said she needed to see the top of my prosthetic as well. I was confused because I hadn't ever had to do that before. I make a habit of wearing tight yoga pants while traveling because they provide pressure on my nubs and are the most comfortable when I need to press the button and release the pin system on my prosthetic legs to adjust. I told her I'd never had to do anything like that before and the only way to get to my knees is by pulling down my pants.

The TSA agent said, "Yeah, you're gonna have to do that."

I was clearly uncomfortable and was trying not to argue but looked around and said, "Where?"

We were in the middle of the airport security area, and there was nowhere private to go in sight. There was a sweet, middle-aged couple behind me, and the wife placed a hand on my shoulder as she told me she was so, so sorry this was happening to me. It was such a small gesture, but it made me feel like I wasn't crazy to be uncomfortable and flustered in that moment.

The TSA agent called another woman agent over, and they took me to a tiny room that looked like an unused storage closet. This room clearly wasn't designed for amputees or anyone who may need to strip down in a safe environment. It was a little room with trash on the floor, water bottles confiscated from people coming through security, some extra chairs, and a desk. It seemed like they'd just chosen a random space that was close by for this private moment.

I asked again why I had to do this when I've never had to before, and the TSA agent kept repeating that this was the protocol and it was always like this. I started asking more questions and was trying to be nice about it but wanted to understand why it was necessary. The TSA agent was rude enough—and I happened to have enough time before my flight that day—that I asked to speak to whomever was in charge. They brought in their head of TSA who had been in a different terminal. He knew who I was, having seen my Super Bowl commercial, and he apologized but told me this was their standard protocol and that it would need to happen. I said, "This is your standard protocol for children, babies, sexual assault survivors, and all people with disabilities?"

In a bizarre attempt to assuage my discomfort, they mentioned a man who'd thrown himself on the floor because he was so upset with their protocol and the process I'd just been through. They were trying to relay that people get upset, but that's their standard protocol anyway—but all I heard was the way they laughed at this man as they talked about how he traveled frequently with them and always threw himself on the floor. I was appalled that they were mocking a man who clearly was distraught or had a cognitive disorder. It felt very dehumanizing all over again. I asked what they suggest for people like that then—for people like me who are uncomfortable. They said, "Don't travel."

Traveling is part of my career, and it sounded like it was part of this man's life as well. Telling someone not to travel because your own protocol is flawed is not okay.

Finally, I agreed to pull down my pants but said calmly that I wouldn't continue until after they'd removed the agent who was being nasty to me. I wasn't going to strip down to my thong in front of her after the way she'd been speaking to me, acting like I was ridiculous for feeling uncomfortable. I felt like I had that power at least. I was left with another woman TSA agent who gave me a cloth to cover myself that was roughly the size of the napkin they pin to your chest at the dentist's office. After she swabbed my leg, I had to stand up to clip into my prosthetics and pull up my pants, so the cloth was basically pointless.

No alarms went off and the process ended, but I still didn't understand why that was their protocol when I had never experienced it in that way before. I was caught off guard by the whole process, but I was more upset for the next person to come through and have to go through that. I have since talked to a friend who I met on the U.S. Paralympic team who said that something similar had happened to her, and it had also been new for her. She reached out to the TSA and shared both of our experiences, and I also reached out to the TSA and gave my story and the information about that gate and who worked there. Nothing really happened as a result, except they told us that it was completely and totally inappropriate and not what they aimed to do. I didn't want to fight so much that they forced every airport to stick to a tougher protocol, but I do think consistency across the board is necessary to make sure screening is done in a careful and humanizing way.

I spoke up during that experience because I didn't like the thought of people having to feel as uncomfortable and confused as I felt. It's okay, and sometimes necessary, to speak up and fight for yourself and others, finding that balance between speaking out and showing kindness. I spoke up for my own emotional safety by asking for the one TSA agent to be removed from the room, and I spoke up for others by asking questions and then sharing my experience. We may not always get huge responses when we speak up, or people saying, "Wow, you're right! Thanks!" But we must choose to advocate for the things that we know to be right.

TIME TO SPEAK UP, OR TIME TO MAINTAIN YOUR OWN PEACE?

Some personalities have to push themselves to speak up, and others have to hold back sometimes and decide what the end goal actually is. I'm a big believer in choosing your battles. I feel things strongly and love to take action. I'm a fighter and always ready to stand up to people if needed, a trait that has been well developed throughout my life, so

I've had to learn how to take a step back and ask myself if it's worth it and what I hope to accomplish. How do we stand in the middle of two extremes and decide which moments require speaking out and in which ones we should prioritize our own emotional safety and well-being over dealing with other people's chosen ignorance?

The human body is amazing, and it's very equipped to *know* when to act. It'll give you signals—these are your instincts, which you should listen to and heed. I feel it in my gut when people are being treated unfairly. Most of us probably experience that sensation but aren't always sure what to do. I know that when it's time to step in and take care of others, it's going to be uncomfortable. I'm going to want to stay quiet, but there's a feeling in the pit of my stomach that tells me I'll regret it later. Even if it feels like you're the only one speaking out or you're not being taken seriously, at least you didn't ignore the issue.

Learning to listen to your body with *discernment,* however, is what will keep you from picking a fight every time you get heated. My body can tell me when I'm too exhausted or fired up to handle a conversation correctly, and it can tell me when it's time to speak up, even though it'll be uncomfortable and my voice might crack. I don't do passive aggression, and I'll say outright what needs to be said. Those around me know I'll always fight for them, and they trust me to speak the truth even when it's hard to hear. Developing your intuition and learning to trust yourself is done through taking action, not through being passive in every situation.

You can't always trust your emotional response, but you can trust that gut feeling and internal sense of knowing. We each may have a different sensation that signals to us, so maybe your first step is to start tuning into your body in those moments you think you should speak up, and pinpoint where and how it's signaling you. Does your heart rate pick up speed as your palms get clammy? Does your body feel warm and your stomach drop? We have to practice listening and distinguishing what information our body is relaying to us, and then have the courage to act on it. It's hard to speak up when it's not something you've ever done. Just like anything else, you get better with practice.

So before you can discern when it's time to speak up or when it's time to focus on maintaining your peace, you have to first ask yourself, *Am I responding from a place of anger or hurt?* For example, I know I need to care for myself first, take a time-out from the conversation, or remove myself altogether when I start assuming people's motives are negative or if it's triggering a prior wound in me to the point where I can't see the forest for the trees. I'll only be responding from a place of anger, which helps no one.

How do you care for your own emotional well-being when you get worked up or when people are rude or insensitive to you? What has helped me the most is reminding myself that the person I need to speak up to is only seeing a piece of the picture; they don't have the whole story or know the details of my life, and vice versa. When you can actually sit down and get to know people and hear their story, their struggle, and what they've been through, it creates empathy and connection between you. It certainly gives you perspective. I'm positive that if I were able to sit down with every single person who has ever judged me, and I shared my story and the pain that I've been through and how hard it can be at times, they wouldn't be as quick to give me a hard time. I think they'd respond with empathy, and we could find the points in our stories where we had the same emotions and similar human thoughts and experiences. When you can appreciate that every single person is going through something, you start to give people the benefit of the doubt and show more compassion.

But the reality is, we don't always have that time with people. When you don't have that time to get to know each other, and people are very quick to judge, you still have to choose maintaining your own emotional peace over all of it. Standing up for what's right is important, but you can't do that well if you're already depleted and just coming from a space of anger and defensiveness. Sometimes the right thing in that moment looks like forcing yourself to walk away instead of reacting. Your own emotional safety and well-being is your responsibility, as is responding from a place of health.

You are not responsible for other people's feelings and responses, only your own. That's a hard sentence to swallow and grasp for anyone used to managing the people around them—for anyone who's averse to confrontation or who finds it difficult to speak up for themselves. And especially for those of us who are dedicated to keeping things lighthearted and calm. But you don't want to be so afraid of possible conflict that you give up pieces of who you are and what you believe in. I'm not saying forget about people's feelings and be irresponsible, doing whatever you want. I'm saying it's up to you to kindly speak your needs and express yourself for who you are, and people's reactions to that are their own responsibility. Likewise, we can take it upon ourselves to share our stories with one another in an effort to educate the people around us, but the responsibility to learn is ultimately our own.

We must resist the urge to cater to other people's feelings out of shame or fear. For example, I don't need to exaggerate my limp just so other people don't get upset that I don't look disabled while using the handicap line. There's a difference between coddling people, or people-pleasing, and being sensitive to other people's feelings and levels of awareness. Yes, be sensitive, but don't feel that you need to coddle them or mollify them. We shouldn't stifle our voices or any piece of who we are out of fear that we'll offend someone, but speaking with kindness from a foundation of self-assuredness and discernment is always the right approach. If that makes people uncomfortable, don't let that shut you down. Instead, pause and ask yourself, *Why do I feel so timid? Why do I shut down?* Own your power, and own the unique experience that you bring to the table.

We have to work on feeling confident enough to show our full selves to the world, especially when that means maintaining our own sense of balance and peace, self-worth and self-esteem. Practicing listening to your body, protecting your peace, and speaking up for yourself and others in the little moments prepares you to have that discernment in the bigger moments that will come later on down the line. We should never want to cater to someone else's needs and feelings if that requires neglecting our own, and we should never neglect other people's needs and feelings because we're only concerned about our own. How we interact with people is about finding and maintaining that balance.

The Reframe

Take a few minutes to decide on a boundary you're going to implement this week. Boundaries are the limits and rules we place around ourselves to protect us. Use that boundary this week to practice speaking up or protecting your peace, and monitor how your body responds. Write down how you felt and where you felt it in your body. This information can eventually help you discern your body's signals for how to handle each situation, even if you hadn't developed a boundary specifically for it.

A boundary idea for you could be, "If anyone around me makes fun of someone, I will calmly state that I don't find unkind remarks funny." Or, "If I get upset with someone in a group setting, I will give myself time to process it and then reach out to that one person directly, without going through third parties." A boundary I've implemented (and am still working on) is, if I ask someone to help me with a task, I can't critique them for getting it done but doing it differently from how I would've done it.

8

Redefining Society

JUST AS WE'RE constantly trying to make sense of the world around us, so are our brains. Our brains are constantly taking in already-processed information from past encounters we've had and things we've learned to help guide us along our way for future interactions. This information that our brains gather is then used to develop patterns that inform us on how to respond to new encounters. In doing so, we create an internal system of *assumptions* based on our past experiences that then inform and carry over into our new experiences. This is how we learn to discern what's dangerous to us and what's not, whom we can trust, or even how to finish our friend's or partner's sentences based on previous encounters and conversations we've had with them. You start to expect what you've seen and heard before in similar situations. This can become dangerous, however, when you start forming expectations and assumptions of others and the world around you based on your own specific experiences—or from hearsay someone else has told you but you haven't ever experienced for yourself.

After experiencing toxicity or trauma in one relationship, we may then carry those developed fears and triggered responses into our later relationships with others. Once there is a story in place, our mind repeats it unless we interrupt the cycle with new information or understandings. I was abandoned as a baby, so even when I was brought into a new, loving family, I assumed and expected that my adopted family would send me back to Russia and abandon me, too. The story in my mind was that I was unlovable, expendable. It took years of seeing my family's consistent love—and years of working toward loving myself—to overcome that childhood fear. Then that fear of abandonment appeared again in my relationship with my husband, Lucas. I went through periods of "testing" him to see if he could handle the worst parts of me, pushing him away because of my own fear that he couldn't *truly* love me because I was not worth loving. When the story in your mind is rooted in your body, causing real symptoms like panic or anxiety that try to protect you from experiencing those traumas again, your actions begin to come from a place of fear, as mine did. I still have moments where I need to interrupt that internal story that I'm unlovable, choosing instead to trust the affection I receive and let it add to the love I have for myself. That's how we start to unlearn and overcome that cycle of bringing our old traumas into new relationships—we have to start believing a different story about ourselves.

Even outside of experiencing any trauma, we make so many little assumptions about people and the world around us based on how we were raised or what we've been told. These assumptions are based on the biases we've developed throughout our lives. Assumptions are guesses we make based on the information we have, while biases are the predisposed narrative that we base our assumptions on. When biases are left unexamined, we can make automatic assumptions without even realizing it.

You'll recall how I've parked my Toyota in handicapped parking only to be stopped numerous times by people who felt I didn't deserve that spot based on my appearance, for example. They've given me annoyed looks and left angry notes on my vehicle, not realizing that I actually do have a disability and need the closer parking. This is all based on their assumptions about what a disabled person should look like. Based on these assumptions, they then judge me in a way that can seem so insignificant to the outside world but starts to add up when it happens often. When we make assumptions about people without stopping to give them the benefit of the doubt, we can create hostile encounters that affect ourselves and each other in ways we never intended.

Stop to consider: What do you assume when you meet someone who looks different from you—whether based on race, ethnicity, weight, tattoos, clothing, or something else? Do you assume that they're not a good person? Do you shun them because you fear people who aren't like you? Or do you understand that our differing life experiences and how we present ourselves to the world are what make us each distinct individuals with something unique to offer society?

I was once in a friend's wedding where people's biases came into play yet again. While the bride allowed some of her bridesmaids to pick their own dresses, she decided to choose dresses for me and our mutual friend. She selected dresses that we both felt were unflattering on us, so we brought up our discomfort with the dresses the next time the three of us had dinner together. The bride expressed that she thought we were beautiful and was surprised that we felt self-conscious at all. Her bias was that people who are considered beautiful by societal standards don't ever feel self-conscious about their bodies. Her assumption based on that bias was that we wouldn't mind having our dresses chosen for us because we'd look good in whatever she picked for us.

Unexamined biases can result in misunderstandings, but they can also result in serious harm done to others. Our biases can cause us to categorize entire groups of people together and make unfair assumptions about them instead of allowing each individual to be seen for who they are. For example, you might assume that all people with disabilities look a certain way or that all people of the same race are the same, not unique individuals with unique stories to tell. If we are to accept people's differences and show kindness to everyone, we can't leave our own biases unaddressed because these very biases are often what hinder us from treating each other as we want to be treated. It's up to each of us to self-reflect and start challenging our own internal biases as we seek to understand the unique experiences of everyone around us. The more we examine *why* we do things and the reasoning behind the assumptions we make, the more we understand ourselves and can make better conscious decisions.

DOES SOCIAL MEDIA IMPACT OUR
BIASES? OF COURSE IT DOES!

Having full awareness over what we say and do is even more important in the age of social media. Your comment or opinion is no longer
just a passing remark witnessed by a few people, but a judgment that's
viewable by the entire world, staying there to be read for years. Even
as *you* learn and grow, challenging the systems of bias and assumptions
you make in your mind, people still have access to your thoughts from
years ago via the comments you've posted. Your words have the power
to hurt you just as much as they can hurt others. Hurt people hurt
people, and that just keeps the cycle going for us all.

Social media has given us access to more voices and experiences outside of our own, creating an opportunity for us to educate ourselves and
expand our circles of understanding, experiences, and areas of influence.
But it has also given us access to a network where the comparison game
and "judging a book by its cover" have thrived, rooting this mentality
into our lives. It has opened up a space where our biases can be shared
with the whole world and has compounded our judgments around what
we find attractive, valuable, and socially acceptable.

What we don't realize is just how much this can affect our own
self-esteem and feelings of self-worth. Just think about your own social
media accounts. Every ad is designed to make us feel like we *need*
that product, making us believe that we'll be prettier, hotter, or stronger if we use or wear that product. Teaching us to dislike ourselves is
how corporations have made money for too long. Remember all those
clothes I bought but never wore as a teenager, all those tubes of expensive mascara and vials of perfume I just had to have? I've spent way
too much money over the years on things that I didn't need, trying to
soothe my own feelings of unworthiness and lack of self-confidence.
So I can tell you that social media (not to mention flashy spending on
products) doesn't change your mindset for the better if you're already
dissatisfied with yourself! We must first heal ourselves—improving our
own understanding of our self-worth—before we can find that true
sense of self-confidence that we often search for online. If we don't

like ourselves, then how can we meaningfully interact and positively engage with the rest of the world?

It's up to us to guard our minds and our hearts from messages that try to deny our own inherent value and self-worth. The bulk of the comments I receive are warm and uplifting, friendly, and grateful for the representation that I've shown for people with disabilities, but I do get comments from people who see my missing legs as a tragedy—or at least as something that makes me less desirable. I receive several messages each week that are all very similar:

"You're pretty for a girl with no legs."

"Wow, you're still beautiful without your legs."

"I'd still date you even without your legs."

"Pretty girl, but I wish she had legs."

Reread those sentences and think about what they're saying. It's taken me a long time to get to where I'm comfortable showing my legs to the world, but I'm still human. Those comments are damaging, hurtful, and painful to encounter. I'm relatively confident in who I am now, but imagine a new amputee or a young girl who's new to social media, showing her prosthetic legs for the first time. Imagine if she received messages like that. I can't imagine what it would have felt like for me if I had social media back when I was thirteen. As a young woman constantly facing such a barrage of backhanded compliments and insults about my appearance, worth, and desirability in my day-to-day life, these comments would have had the power to cause immeasurable emotional damage if I had received them upon bravely showing my legs after years of struggling to be comfortable doing so.

THE DARK SIDE OF BEAUTY BIAS

We must change the narrative that people with a disability are less pretty, less "normal," or less valuable to society. We're all different, and our differences don't take away from our worth, whether we're fully able-bodied or not. Yet, many of the comments I receive, particularly on social media, insinuate that I'm automatically considered "less than" because I'm missing something. Those words insinuate that I'm not whole. But who gets to decide what "pretty" is and what we value as attractive and socially acceptable in our society?

We have all been bombarded with standards of beauty since the moment we were born. Those societal beliefs have led us to develop biases that equate attractiveness or wholeness to mean "without a disability." Remember how my parents had to cut off the legs of my dolls, so that they would look more like me, and how I never saw anyone who looked like me until I was well into my amputee journey? For years, the only beauty representation that I saw told me that people who looked like me were odd, that we weren't as desirable as those without disabilities. The people who leave me these comments probably don't even realize the negative effects that their words could have—not just on me but on anyone, including other people with disabilities who are reading those words. That's what happens when your biases are left unexamined. You hurt others and show yourself to be inconsiderate and ill-informed about the world.

We can claim to support people with disabilities—running in 5Ks to support disabilities and protesting the ill treatment of those who have them—but if we still see people who are differently abled as "less than" someone who doesn't have a disability, whether that means less attractive or less valuable to society, then we're missing the entire point. Maybe we can't help what we were taught and what lessons seeped in before we knew better and learned to examine our own biases. But we *can choose* now what we allow to stay in our minds and within our behavior, asking ourselves what we believe and why.

The majority of people in the world aren't missing limbs, but that doesn't make those of us who are any less normal or valuable in society. According to the World Health Organization (WHO), an estimated 1.3 billion people—or 16 percent of the global population—experienced a significant disability in 2023.[1] That's 1.3 billion people who are capable and strong. We are beautiful. We are valuable. We are able.

I've spent most of my life going back and forth on whether I fully believe all of those things about myself—that I'm capable and strong, beautiful, valuable, and able. It has been an ongoing process to love myself and maintain my confidence, to remind myself of all that my body has done for me and that my worth is inherent and unrelated to how I look or perform. You may not be missing any limbs or have a disability, you may not be adopted or an athlete, but I believe we can all identify with having a piece of ourselves that we're self-conscious about. Think about any insecurities you have that make you feel defensive when they're pointed out or callously remarked upon. We all have them.

These negative remarks often stay with us. They scar us and emotionally deform us. We're now experiencing more mental health issues and depression than ever before as a country. According to the CDC, the overall suicide rate increased 30 percent between 2000 and 2020.[2] That's the damage of people feeling alone and *othered*, the same feelings I've felt at times throughout my life. In so many ways, this is representative of an amalgamation of undiagnosed mental illness, toxic environments, discrimination, and social media anxiety that have had a damaging impact on us, both individually and collectively. The first time my mom mentioned therapy to me as a teenager, I told her I'd kill my therapist if she got me one. I was full of emotional anxiety and anger and was on the road to battling depression later in my life. I must have said it with just enough conviction, because she never tried to make me speak to anyone. I never thought I'd be the girl who went to therapy. I thought therapy was for the weak, and I never wanted to be weak. But here I am, having been in therapy for the past six years, and I need it every week. It has made me stronger, more compassionate, and more aware of the areas where I need to grow. And so much of that emotional pain that I saved up was from the emotional impact of negative remarks and experiences in my life.

Do you have a hurtful memory like this that you've been holding on to for years, whether it was an intentionally mean comment or question hurled your way, or an innocent remark about that thing that makes you most self-conscious? I hope your memory is short for the negative things and long for the positive, but it's important to understand that most people who make comments to us don't *realize* they're hurtful, even when they are. It took me years to come to understand this. Comments like, "You're an inspiration," just because I left my house to run errands, or, "You're beautiful even though you don't have legs," are hurled my way by people thinking that they're being nice, but who are actually triggering a deep fear within me that I don't belong and will always be *other*. That's why it's important to think twice before speaking or posting comments. You never know who you'll affect with them and how deeply they can cut.

In order for us to create change in the world, we must first understand the social systems that determine the "value," "attractiveness," and "acceptability" of people, and we must learn to question those systems. I see how people are nicer to me when I'm all done up versus when I'm barefaced and rolling in from a workout. Not only do I receive more free stuff when my hair and makeup are done, but even the way people engage with me is different. It's like suddenly people seem more interested and drawn to me just because they think I'm attractive. This differing treatment based on appearance has been named *beauty bias* or the *halo effect*. People who are considered more attractive by society are also assumed to be more trustworthy, to be more confident, and to have better social skills. They're assumed to be more intelligent in some scenarios as well.[3] When we judge someone's character based on our impression of their physical appearance, that's beauty bias. Statistically, people who are considered attractive get called back for more job interviews, make more money, and receive more lenient jail sentences.[4] Depending on how I present myself and who the audience is, I've seen the benefits of being considered a "pretty blonde," while also experiencing people assuming that I'm ditzy or a pushover—that is, until I show them that I have sides beyond sweet and bubbly. Society says I'm incomplete and *other*, both privileged *and* disadvantaged depending on the situation, but I know I'm more than my body, my looks, and what I can offer the world. We cannot allow ourselves to be reduced to "just bodies," to just labels that others place upon us. We're more than what's on the outside.

USING OUR PRIVILEGE TO BE A VOICE FOR CHANGE

I've felt anger, rejection, and confusion at how the world has viewed me, even going so far as to crop my pictures above the knees so my legs never showed in the images I'd post to social media, just to avoid being seen as different. Yet I've also felt empowered by my own body and experiences. I've felt that I can make a difference being an amputee. I've felt joy, gratefulness, and confidence in how I'm different. Just like everyone else, I've felt just about every emotion under the sun, even though I'm missing my legs. We all have a connection to all of these same emotions, even if we have lived experiences that other people don't understand. If we can understand these emotions within ourselves, then we can begin to understand them in each other. We all have struggles living in this world, society, culture, or space—especially those of us who are marginalized, for whom the world wasn't initially built with us in mind.

No one should ever be discriminated against for anything that may make them different from those around them. As much of a cliché as it is, you never truly know a person until you've walked a mile—or a lifetime—in their shoes. Our stories are more complex than what others may assume they know about us at first glance. So, how do you remind yourself to look outside of the physical and what you're capable of to understand your inherent value? Once we can remind ourselves that *we* are inherently valuable, then we can also do this for others. That is the first step to seeing that everyone on the planet has worth to our societies. How can we create collective change for people who experience discrimination based on their size, shape, abilities, sexual orientation, and skin color? It's about knowing and understanding our challenges as well as knowing and understanding our privilege.

Holding privilege doesn't mean your life is easy or that you haven't faced struggles; it just means the way our society was built does not make things even harder for you. Everyone can hold privilege in one area or another in their lives. I'm an amputee in a society that was built for "able-bodied" individuals. I have to think about how much walking I'll have to do when I travel to different places, or if there will be cobblestones or uneven ground where I'll struggle to balance. I know what it's like to be in a wheelchair after surgeries and have to think about and ask people if locations are wheelchair accessible—you'd be surprised by how many are not. These are disadvantages to me that make me different from most other people. However, I'm also a young, white, middle-class, heterosexual, blonde woman who is viewed as attractive in our society. I know that this has helped me get everything from contracts for ad campaigns to features in magazines—options that I may not have been given the privilege to experience if I didn't fall under some of those categories. When you're privileged, you get advantages and options that others do not, simply because you *are* of that privileged group of people—not necessarily because you deserve it based on your merits more than anyone else does. Though my life hasn't been easy and I *am* at a perceived disadvantage for having a disability, I still have to acknowledge the privilege that I *do* have that gives me advantages over others in different ways every day.

Race, gender, socioeconomic status, health, parentage . . . these are all part of who we are, and you should never have to apologize for any of it. That said, you're not paying very much attention if you can't see how society favors one side, or group, from all of these areas. In our society, being a white, cisgender, heterosexual, wealthy man will give you all the advantages our society has to offer, particularly if you're young (so you don't face ageism) and good looking (which gives you the benefit of beauty bias). That's not a statement meant to make anyone feel guilty; it's just an acknowledgment that our society was built by men like them *for* men like them. Coming together with our unique stories, gifts, and insights is how we thrive—as an individual, a family, a company, a society, and a world. Awareness of our biases helps us to understand society's biases. Awareness of society's biases helps us to understand our own areas of privilege. And awareness of our own areas of privilege helps us to know where our voices carry more weight because of our privilege, so we can use our voices to advance and amplify those that are being ignored.

My success in swimming has given me a platform where people listen to what I have to say. It's my responsibility to do something good with that. I don't want to get to the end of my life knowing that there were people who were hurting, or people who didn't have a voice because society told them they weren't enough, and realize that I didn't use the platform God gave me to speak and advocate for them. You may not be a professional athlete or feel like you have a platform, but you have coworkers, family, or friends that were placed in your life. It's your responsibility to use your voice in your circles and area of influence for good and positive change. Don't waste it.

Even if you don't think you're having an impact, small moments create the momentum for big changes. Change starts with us. It starts with you. We can shift cultures by taking personal accountability for our part, by understanding what we have to offer our societies to make them better, and then by bringing that into our communities and working to build a better future. This is how we shift cultures.

The more we acknowledge and accept our differences, and stop approaching those who are different from ourselves with an "us versus them" mentality, the more change we can create. Sometimes that small moment is saying the hard or uncomfortable things. Sometimes it's listening and amplifying other voices that need to be heard instead of our own. When we address our biases and stop making those who aren't like us feel *othered*, we can connect with one another and start addressing the systems of power that elevate certain groups of people over others.

My story will always be more powerful coming from me, and your story will always be more powerful coming from you. If someone feels equipped enough to use their voice to address their own experience, it's better for us to support them instead of trying to jump into the conversation with less insight. When we bring awareness to these topics, putting our own experiences with privilege and bias out in the open, it can no longer be ignored and must be addressed. When we share our experiences, we connect through our similarities and gain more understanding for our differences. Let's continue to make it the norm for people to look, speak, and act in their own unique way, bringing our one-of-a-kind insights and experiences to the table.

You have every right to take up space. You have every right to be in the room. So do I—even if when I walk into a room, whether I like it or not, people are going to look at me. When you walk into a room, maybe you're the person everyone's looking at because you're different. And even if you don't recognize it, that's a really special power. It may not always feel like a positive thing, and it can be exhausting at times, but you hold attention in a way that's unique. Own your differences without trying to hide them—a lesson that it took me so many years to learn. Own and love who you are, then start championing others to do the same. Champion others to challenge society to alter its systems, beliefs, and biases. If you're different from others, from the societal norms of your community in any way, then people are going to look at you. Give them something to look at. Let's give them a new perspective.

The first step in dismantling our biases and assumptions—confronting the harmful narratives that our societies and social media have perpetuated—is acknowledging *you*. Maybe that means acknowledging your past. Maybe that means acknowledging where you came from and the journey you've been on to get where you are now. Maybe that means acknowledging the hurt that feels like it's a part of you. Even if your story didn't start in a great place—maybe you've come from a place of abandonment and feeling unlovable like mine—know that that's not the end of your story. You have so many more pages to write. The more you unravel the pieces of yourself, the more you can reflect on how your journey has impacted the way you view the world. The more we reflect, the more we're able to connect with people and the more we're able to understand that not everything we've been taught by society as the "norm" is okay. It's time for us to stand up and start doing the work to alter our world for the better. Through our own self-acceptance and empathy for each other's differences, fighting for growth and change in ourselves and in the spaces we inhabit, we can redefine the society we want to live in.

The Reframe

We are each more than one thing. Our lived realities are shaped by different factors and social dynamics operating together. You may experience discrimination or marginalization in one area, or in multiple overlapping areas of life. You may also experience discrimination in one area and privilege in another, just as I've faced ableism but also benefited from beauty bias. Take a few minutes to think about your life and answer these questions:

1. What factors of who I am have made my life harder than it is for other people?

2. What factors of who I am have made my life easier than it is for other people? This doesn't have to be extreme. If you inherently "fit in" in your workplace, neighborhood, and so on, then you possess some sort of privilege.

3. How can I use my privilege from my answer to the second question to help welcome and advocate for others?

Helping others to be equally seen and heard can start with something as simple as introducing the new person at work or reading a book that shares a completely different perspective from an author you wouldn't normally gravitate toward. *Privilege* is not an offensive word. It's simply recognizing the areas in which you can help while facing the least resistance. So, let's help each other!

9

Representation Matters

"JESS, THIS IS for you."

I remember my dad bringing in the mail as he came home from work one day. He handed me an envelope addressed to me as I was at the kitchen table doing my homework. I was eight years old, and I usually only got letters on my birthday, so my curiosity was piqued as I tore into it. It was a note from a prosthetic company where I'd had a recent appointment in our search for a new prosthetist, along with an advertising brochure card. But what caught my attention was the beautiful blonde woman on the front of the card, leaning back on her elbows with her *two prosthetic legs* propped on the wall in front of her. They were C-shaped running-blade legs, not legs covered in skins like mine. At that age, I only wore realistic-looking prosthetic legs, not yet confident enough to wear legs that would more obviously label me as different from everyone else. But she wasn't hiding anything and looked proud of who she was as she stared directly into the camera, directly at me. Her name was printed at the bottom of her photo: Aimee Mullins.

It felt like I was seeing a glimpse of myself fifteen years in the future, and I had to know more about her. I immediately asked my dad about this woman on the front of this brochure card. Who *was* she? Why did *she* look like me? I asked my dad, and he did some research; he was just as curious as I was. We found out Aimee was also born with fibular hemimelia, the same birth defect I had, and she had become a model, actor, and athlete.

I spent hours staring at that picture in amazement. My dad and I used to call those running legs "cheetah legs," and he'd tell me that I could get some if I wanted them and run faster than anyone else. But we had to be very careful with my knees at that point in my life. I was going through surgeries every few months, so I wasn't a hundred percent stable, and it didn't really make sense to get a pair of cheetah legs made and then go in for another surgery, making me unable to fit into those legs. That was always the challenge—the unpredictability of my surgeries and the infections that I might go through afterward. So, I didn't actually run for the first time until I was fifteen years old, years after I'd won my first Paralympic gold medal. We later discovered that I didn't have the ligaments in my knees that I need for running—and that running could damage my knees enough to permanently put me in a wheelchair—yet I held onto that picture of the brave woman who looked like me. I saved that picture for years, sometimes just sitting on my bed staring at it. It served as a reminder to me that I wasn't alone.

Before I joined the Paralympics and was able to see all those athletes—athletes who looked like me—out on the pool deck, there were two people who impacted me and made me feel less alone in my journey. Aimee was one of them—a bilateral, below-the-knee amputee who was beautiful and fierce and exactly how I wanted to be. The second person was Rudy Garcia Tolson, whom I spotted when I was eleven years old on one of those "Check This Kid Out" segments on the Disney Channel. Rudy was a bilateral, above-the-knee amputee who'd also been born with a cleft lip and palate, a combination of both me and my brother, Josh, who was adopted from Russia alongside me. Rudy was born with several defects in his legs that made them unusable, and after having fifteen surgeries by the age of five, he told his parents that he would rather be an amputee. I was watching the Disney Channel at my grandparents' house and felt this surge of hope and amazement as I saw Rudy with no legs, skateboarding, running, swimming, and doing all of these things just like other kids, just like me. His story was powerful; it moved me, awed me.

That's the power of representation: *connection*, showing someone they're not alone. Aimee and Rudy gave me hope that I could do exactly what my stubborn spirit was already trying to convince me I could do: absolutely anything I wanted. These were two important moments in my life because I saw both Aimee and Rudy before I had competitive swimming. I hadn't yet seen other bilateral amputees out in the world. My family, friends, and neighbors all had two legs. My Barbies had two legs. Even the My Twinn doll that my parents had gotten me for Christmas when I was nine or ten years old, which was supposed to look exactly like me, had disappointed me by having two legs—so, in fact, *unlike* me. I remember being so upset when I pulled her out of the box and saw that she wasn't missing her legs like I was. Everyone around me had legs, so seeing other young, bilateral amputees out there, living their lives and being adventurous and competitive, not letting anything hold them back, resonated with a part of me that I hadn't been sure anyone could fully understand. I remember those moments meaning so much to me. It's easier to recognize the power in our differences when we see other people owning and utilizing their own differences.

Months after first seeing Rudy on TV, I showed up to the pre-competition training for my first national Paralympic meet at eleven years old, intimidated and nervous. All the lanes in the pool were open for all the different classifications of swimmers, and I breathed in the smell of the chlorine and the sound of lightly splashing water as many of the athletes warmed up for their events. I spotted Rudy on the edge of the pool. He'd just hopped out, finishing up his training before his meet started. He still had on his cap and goggles, with his goggles pulled up onto his forehead, and I recognized him right away. I leaned over to my dad and said, "Look! There's the Disney Channel kid!" Little did I know that only two years later, I would get my own "Check That Kid Out" segment on the Disney Channel when I was thirteen years old! That Disney commercial was the first time I got to be a representative for this community of athletes and people with disabilities, but even then, I didn't fully realize how *I* had become that same representation for others that Rudy had been to me.

We didn't have cable at our house, so I only saw my segment aired once or twice at my grandparents' house, and we also received a copy of it from the producers. At the time, I had a few friends who saw it, but this was before our world of social media. So I never realized how many people had watched me on their televisions thinking, *Check that kid out!* It wasn't until I posted part of the segment to my TikTok in January 2021, over 15 years after the Disney segment originally aired, that the comments came flooding in. People were tagging friends and reminiscing on how that video had impacted them: "I thought you were the coolest girl! I loved your puka shell necklace!" I didn't even know people would remember—or that they had had those responses as kids. When I posted that video, I was in COVID isolation before I could go back to training, so the outpouring of positive reactions really warmed my heart and spirit.

I became an ambassador for Team USA when I joined the Paralympic team at twelve years old. I had *just* found my community and was starting down my journey of self-acceptance, and it's incredible to me that even at that point in my life my story was impacting people. I wasn't yet making public statements or advocating for causes, but, looking back, that experience taught me that you never know how simply showing up and being yourself will affect people. I bet that, at first, Rudy didn't realize how he was affecting other amputees either.

Rudy and I have competed in every Paralympic Games together since both making the team for Athens 2004, and we became friends while living and training at the U.S. Olympic and Paralympic Training Center (USOPTC) in Colorado Springs for the two years I was out there. I got to meet Aimee, too, at a red carpet event in 2007, when I was just a young teenager. She knew who I was when I went up to her, and I thought that was the coolest thing. I got to tell her how much that picture and her story meant to me as a child, and we now remain in contact. That was huge for me, getting to meet and become friends with these people who were my heroes as a young girl.

Before I had the Paralympics and an entire team of athletes like me—people who had disabilities, had been adopted, had crazy stories, and understood all of those hidden parts of me—I just had a picture of Aimee and a Disney commercial featuring Rudy. They gave me hope, and then everyone in the Paralympics showed me that I had an entire community with me. I looked around at that first meet, where I spotted Rudy, and thought, *Oh my gosh, there are more of us out there. Where have they all been hiding?* That was the true beginning of this journey of owning who I am and not resenting what makes me unique. That's the power of having a community.

Back then, social media as we know it now didn't yet exist. You couldn't find entire groups of people who related to you just by clicking on a hashtag, so those glimpses of community as a child impacted me greatly. That's why we need more of it. We need more people with disabilities in advertisements, in magazines, on television, and in the entertainment industry because there's always a little girl or boy out there watching who may not even realize yet that they're looking for someone who looks just like them. We should see representation of all the beautiful colors and sizes, cultures and abilities, that make up the whole of who we are as one giant community of humanity. What could that look like for the future?

THE VALUE OF COMMUNITY

Having my friends from Team USA has changed my life. There's a sense of hope and connection in seeing someone who looks like you who's succeeding or doing the thing you want to do one day, but getting to walk alongside these incredible athletes who *get me* fills me with a sense of community that I can't picture doing life without.

I took a hot yoga class once after I hadn't been in a class for a long time, so I was struggling with some of the positions as I adjusted the movements to what I could do on my knees. I'm so used to adapting, and it usually doesn't bother me, but that day it did.

At the end of class, the instructor said to me in total amazement, "You just adapted to everything! I'm so impressed!"

And I thought, *Well, what else was I going to do? I've been adapting my whole life. You think an hour-long yoga class is going to stop me now?*

Afterward, I called up my friend, Julia, who is also an amputee, and told her about hot yoga and how that day was just one of those days where I was frustrated and didn't want to deal with being different. She responded, "Oh, I know, right? Those happen to me, too!" And we ended that call laughing together.

It's the little things—like venting about a problem that's unique to a community and knowing the other person can completely relate—that make us each feel seen and understood. Whether we realize it or not, we all seek out our own communities in this way—those who understand us and where we are in this season of our lives or struggles. We weren't designed to be alone; we all need community and connection.

Community is not just your neighborhood or who sits around you at work. It is the people you choose to place around yourself in your life, whether that is your family or the people you've chosen to call family. It's the people who love all the different sides of you, and the people who truly understand what you've been through or are going through. Sometimes a "me too" is all we need to feel understood or okay again.

The thing is, in order to be fully known and understood for who we are, we have to show up fully as we are. When we see others like us and have that representation, it gives us the courage to say, *If she can do it, I can do it.* There is validation in representation that says, *I'm not alone.* And once you start embracing your differences and showing up as your true self, you can start attracting the people who love and choose you for who you are. That's how you find your community. People can't connect with you if you're hiding.

I know it can be scary to be the first to reach out and put yourself out there. It's easier to convince ourselves that we can do it all alone. Trust me, I've tried to pretend I don't need people, and I've even had myself pretty well convinced. But eventually a season comes and shows you just how much you need people who can help lift you up or just sit with you in understanding. None of us is alone, and as we do the work to accept ourselves and start showing up with transparency, we'll start finding our authentic community. I know that one person can make a difference. But a whole community of people can change the world.

More often than not, what's holding many of us back from sharing our stories is fear. Fear of being judged and rejected or even being fully seen for who we are. But the world needs your story. It's through your story that others will feel seen and validated. It's how others will start to feel safe in their own identities. If we can overcome our fear, we might be able to be the representation the world so needs.

Fear is a very real emotion, and there are certainly times when it may not be safe to show your full authentic self. Unfortunately, we live in a very volatile world, but my hope is that the more we can all show our full selves, the more accepting our world will become.

When I'm feeling the pang of fear take over, I use these three steps to move through it and decide if my fear should be heeded or if it's just there because of old wounds and feelings of rejection.

1. Name the fear. Say it out loud if you're alone. It's real, and you're allowed to be afraid. But just because it's real doesn't mean it can hurt you.

2. Think of the possible outcomes. What's the worst-case scenario?

3. What are the positives or benefits of following through with it anyway?

Whenever I am nervous or afraid, let's say, to post something about my legs to social media—wondering if it's silly or finding things to critique in my appearance—I do this exercise. I name and acknowledge my feelings and fears. Then I think about the worst-case scenario, which is possibly receiving negative comments or mean messages that confirm my own insecurities. And then I think about the potential positives. Someone out there could feel less alone. Someone could be exposed to the world of disability or prosthetics, shared in a positive and empowering way. When the possible benefits outweigh the worst case, it helps you to ease past the fear.

USING SOCIAL MEDIA AS A TOOL

For all of the negative that social media can offer, one of the things I enjoy most about it is how it has started to normalize people having different experiences in life. It gives glimpses into different communities that you may not have experienced otherwise, and it can even be a place to learn about and connect with your own. You can curate your feed to show you differing opinions and diversity in information and lifestyles, if you choose to. It has been a great platform for many people to offer representation when it has been so desperately needed.

A big moment of breakthrough for me was when I posted a video of me putting on my legs and explaining how I do it. I'd hit a wall where I was just tired of people not understanding amputees, tired of the hostile looks I got when I parked in handicapped spaces or even when I wore my bone legs, which I didn't feel confident enough to wear until I was twenty-four. It was in September 2020, and it was only the second TikTok video I'd ever posted. The video jumped to one million views, then six million, all within just a few days. It continued to climb to over thirty-seven million views. It was just a quick video that I decided to post because I hadn't seen any videos like that yet. I had no idea the responses I would get. The questions from people genuinely wanting to learn more and asking for more videos was encouraging. I'd get messages from new amputees saying how much it helped them and empowered them to see me confidently living my life and normalizing doing these everyday tasks as someone with a disability—those moments that most people don't get to see. And if I can inspire just one person, or help one amputee out there to feel understood, then that little ten-second video of me walking in my prosthetics, or the minute-long video of me explaining how I put on my legs, is so worth it.

It was also through social media that I got to meet a sweet little girl named Myah. Myah has spina bifida, and she wears ankle braces and uses crutches or a wheelchair when needed. Her mom posted her reaction to my Team Toyota Super Bowl commercial in 2021, when Myah was only two and a half years old, saying that Myah's face lit up as she said, "That girl has crutches like me!" She then crawled over to grab her crutches, stood up, and said, "I want to be like that girl."

I've had the opportunity to video chat with Myah, and I met her in person about a year after her mother first reached out to me. She hugged me with all her three-year-old might and chatted with me like we were good friends. She decided she trusted me because we were the same, and that really solidified to me what this journey through my life has always been about: helping children all over the world to feel seen. When you feel like you're alone, life can be difficult and challenging. But moments like this made me realize that we are never really alone. There are so many different people out there who may look up to you, who may be looking to you to lead them, whether you realize it or not. That's why it's so important to share your story when you can.

Spending time with Myah took me back to my little self, thinking that there was no one like me. It took me back to how seeing Aimee Mullins's picture completely enthralled me and shifted my view of the world. There are so many of us, so many people who look like we do and feel like we do, even when we navigate this world thinking we're all alone. But in these moments, the big picture—the purpose of my life that had felt elusive to me for many years—became so clear. And I saw, yet again, the reason why representation is important and necessary.

In 2022, A Step Ahead Prosthetics partnered with American Girl and made a Jessica Long doll with two prosthetic legs! They gave me two dolls—one for me to keep and one to gift to someone else. I gave the second doll to Myah, who promptly named her doll after me and started telling everyone that her friend Jessica Long gave it to her. Her mom shared a picture of Myah standing next to her two American Girl dolls, one holding crutches like Myah and one wearing two prosthetic legs like me. Myah was getting to experience something I'd longed for as a child. The power of representation is children seeing glimpses of themselves, knowing that they're not alone, and seeing that their dreams are possible. This is such an important part of how we build our self-identities and our self-esteem; it's a vital stepping stone to understanding our own self-worth. In finding the confidence to share our stories, we get the opportunity to be individuals that the little Myahs of the world can look up to.

WE'RE BETTER THAN THAT, MORE THAN THAT

Being that representation for people is so important to me because I know what they're up against moving through our ableist world. It's not just the comments of "What's wrong with her?" from strangers—you don't realize the little things that aren't readily available to people with disabilities unless you're able to spend several days with us. Sometimes, I see an elevator or handicapped changing room at a retail store being used as storage, which takes away accessibility for those who really need them. These businesses aren't considering the ableist world that we live in, and they aren't considering how a person in a wheelchair may need those accommodations to safely or comfortably get around. Sometimes doors aren't big enough for wheelchair entry or there's no ramp for wheelchair accessibility, which tells people with disabilities that we aren't welcome there. The pool where I'm currently training doesn't have a device to help lower someone into the water who can't walk down the steps, and I know families that have to jump through hoops to get their insurance companies to pay for prosthetics for their children or fight to get skins instead of pole legs. But these are stories that we don't often hear about.

I've been fortunate enough through my swimming career to partner with my prosthetic companies and try different sets of legs. I had the freedom to have realistic-looking painted skins until I was confident enough to be ready to also wear bone legs. Throughout my life up to that point, I tried running legs, rock-climbing legs, and high-heeled legs as I explored my capabilities and felt ready for each pair. This allowed me to, in some ways, hide my disabilities—the pain, discomfort, and aspects of it that made me visibly different from those around me.

In 2019, I did an ad for Tommy Hilfiger that was meant to highlight and celebrate diversity by featuring people with disabilities. In that ad, there was a person in a wheelchair, someone missing one leg, a little girl whose arm stopped at her elbow, and a little boy with a walker. In the photo, I'm sitting in the front, and while you could tell I had prosthetics, you'd have to be looking really hard to be sure—because they were my prosthetic legs that looked like real legs. I remember thinking to myself,

I'm part of this amazing group of people with disabilities, and sometimes I still hide mine to the best of my ability.

After years of hiding and fighting to understand my own self-worth and need for self-acceptance, that was where everything clicked. I thought to myself, *They're not ashamed of their disabilities, so why am I?* That was the year, at twenty-four years old, I got my first set of bone legs. That was the year I finally started showing off my legs on a regular basis, wearing shorts and dresses when I went out. I never thought in my whole life I would be comfortable wearing legs like these, but honestly, I've never felt more confident in showing them off. I was able to take my time getting to that point of comfortability. But I realize that other people haven't had the same advantages and privileges that I had, to be able to blend in until I was ready not to.

I hate that that's not the case for so many people I talk to, some who are new amputees and have to wear pole legs—different from my bone legs, but similar-looking enough that half the time I mistakenly refer to my prosthetics as pole legs—and are told to just be grateful they can walk. There's nothing wrong with pole legs, and I've had friends who get cool designs and love them, but that's what they *chose*. It's much harder to love something when you don't get a choice. We all care about what clothes and shoes we put on each day, about having the *choice* in how we want to express ourselves, and that's the same choice that an amputee deserves when choosing what leg they want to put on and how to present themselves. If everyone had to be in a wheelchair for a week or wear prosthetics, the world would be a very different place, and prioritizing how people with disabilities are accommodated would change very quickly.

Outside of those with physical disabilities, there are also many neurological differences that are ignored by our society; just as bad, people are shamed for them. Research suggests that up to 15 to 20 percent of the U.S. population is neurodivergent,[1] yet we make it a fight for children in schools to get the help they need when they don't learn in the way the school system has been set up to instruct. We all have our strengths and weaknesses, and thankfully, I was able to work at my own pace while being homeschooled. Yet, I have a cousin whose parents fought for years to get her an individualized education program (IEP) to teach her in the way her brain learns and to accommodate how she needs to take tests. My youngest sister, Grace, works with children with autism spectrum disorder (ASD) and attention-deficit/hyperactivity disorder (ADHD) who are struggling in school and socially because they don't have the correct resources available to them. School systems don't adjust to how they learn and interact or help them work through their anger at feeling so different and confused. It's hard to find the right answers, and it's even harder to implement them when that's not the way our school systems and society as a whole are set up. But we can start with educating each other, advocating for more representation, and challenging systems that hinder us instead of helping.

When we fight the system, we might be afraid of being labeled as "difficult" or "complainers," but challenging the way things have always been done is how we progress. Don't let anyone push a label on you—like "dumb blonde" or "disabled girl," as people once labeled me. These labels only stifle what you have to offer the world, making you feel that you can never be anything else. The labels we carry should only be words that *we* choose for ourselves, but too often we get stuck in a box created by the unwanted labels that *other* people place on us. Or, worse, sometimes we start to use those outside labels from others as an excuse to *not* try to reach our full potential.

"Oh I'm ____, so I'm never good at things like that."

"Well, others will just have to deal with that part of my personality because I'm ____."

We adopt labels and use them to explain away our choices. So much of life is out of our control, but we still get to decide how we respond to our circumstances and who we are in the midst of them.

I'm an amputee, an adoptee, a swimmer, a motivational speaker, a woman, an advocate, and a wife. I could list several more labels, from facets of my personality to experiences of my life. They're all parts of who I am, but no label fully describes me—and certainly no label is an excuse to hold me back. I'm not a victim to my circumstances. *We're* not victims to our circumstances, and we can't allow ourselves to be reduced to whatever labels other people may place on us. If a label is ever placed on you by others or yourself, and the label stifles your growth or shames you, then disregard it. It's not meant for you. We're better than that, more than that.

Words are powerful. Remember that old saying about sticks and stones? Whatever. Words hurt, too! I can tell you I've had more positive words and interactions directed toward me than negative, but I still remember that girl when I was twelve years old who told me haughtily that she felt sorry for me. I'll never forget the child at McDonald's who told me to get away from her, so she didn't catch my disease. There are words that have been said to you that you'll never forget. But those words and labels are not yours to carry around and be burdened by. I am not diseased, and I am not to be pitied. What I am is determined to encourage others and be part of a community that wants to normalize our differences, so other kids don't have to have encounters like I did.

Let's not shush children when they have questions, as if our differences are shameful, but teach children about assistive devices (wheelchairs, walkers, crutches, prosthetics, and so on) and how to ask questions politely. I remember a time when I went to train at a pool, and there was a group of young boys there for a swim camp who spotted me. One said, "That's so weird!" while pointing at my legs.

Before I could say anything, another boy spoke up, "No, it's not! That's awesome!" Let's change the narrative of differences being *weird* to being *awesome*.

When I'm feeling insecure or like I want to hide from the curious or hostile glances and comments, I remind myself of that little girl who first held that picture of Aimee Mullins and felt less alone. That has become a standard practice for me—visualizing my younger self. Sometimes that little Russian orphan reminds me of what I love about swimming—to focus less on the sore muscles and more on the freedom I feel as I push my body toward a greater goal. And sometimes that little girl—my younger self—reminds me of what I needed in those years, so I can respond by becoming that very thing for someone else. I needed to see others like me growing up. I needed my differences to be normalized. I needed understanding and connection. So, I want to represent the disabled community and proudly share who I am, reaching out to others.

There are so many little changes that can make big differences. Like holding a picture of someone who is just like you or putting an amputee on the Disney Channel. Representation is an important step in creating change, but let's not stop there! Let's keep showing up and speaking up, as a community, to address the lack of accessibility and change people's perspectives through education and representation. Labels and systems don't get to hold us back or define the way we live our lives. Let's continue striving to normalize our differences and push for a world that adapts alongside us. And remember, *you are not alone.*

The Reframe

If you stop and think about that little girl or boy you used to be, how does that affect the choices you make today?

Will you speak more kindly to yourself when you remember you're also speaking to them?

Will you be more present with your children, remembering how you once felt unheard?

Will you give your dream a chance as you remember how much joy it brought you before the world convinced you not to try?

Will you become softer, bolder, or more determined as you try to make your past self proud?

After you've spent some time thinking about these questions, write a letter to your past self at the time it would have benefited you the most. Maybe during the time you felt most alone and needed to hear that you would someday have a community. Or maybe as the kid who needed to hear that you are valued and have a purpose. I would say to myself, "Jess, it's okay to be angry. It's okay to be a fighter. That's exactly how you made all your biggest dreams come true. But know that it's okay to rest and let go, too. Know that there are so many incredible people out there who look just like you. You are not alone, and you are more than enough."

IO

In the Name of Legacy

"I STILL REMEMBER the days I prayed for the things I have now." Many of you have probably seen a version of that quote somewhere online, or maybe hanging on someone's wall—but how many of us actually take the time to remember those days?

It's easy to get so caught up in our goals for the future, or our current problems, that we forget to be grateful for the things in our lives that we used to only dream about. It's easy to start taking something for granted once you get used to it being there. Swimming is now my job, but it can start to feel like a burden at times, something I'm forcing myself to continue, if I forget about why I started—if I forget about what's at the heart of my love for the sport and for the water.

How do we stay grateful? How do we remember our *why* and not get lost in discontentment as we elevate our goals to the next level? As we advocate for change and challenging any system, how do we keep from burning out?

In a typical week for me, I am traveling to a swim meet, a speech that I'm giving, or an event held by one of my sponsor partnerships. When I'm home in Maryland, I swim in the morning and do Pilates or weight training in the afternoon, and I try to find a pool if I'm away for more than one night. It can feel exhausting, traveling so much along with having phone calls, posting content to social media, connecting with my sports agent, trying to have a social life, and sharing quality time with my husband and family. I can easily start to feel so overwhelmed that I want to avoid the very things that I used to dream about getting to do. I used to swim *for fun*, and now I get paid to do it. I have the opportunity to engage with some incredible people at the events that I attend and share my story to encourage and inspire thousands of people. But when you're exhausted, it's so easy to forget this.

When I think back to the beginning, back to those first steps that brought me to where I am now, I remember that I was an angry girl who found solace in the water. I wasn't thinking about future success as I swam those first few laps and struggled to get across the pool. I did it to channel my thoughts and energy into pushing myself to my limits, and I loved seeing my progress. I did it because I loved a challenge and the feeling of the water as it blocked out all the noise of the outside world. Later, once I found competitive team swimming, I also loved being part of a team and a community that didn't see me as "different," as I quickly started swimming as fast as—and then faster than—anyone else.

After twenty years of training, it makes sense that my feelings sometimes fluctuate on how swimming has become such a big part of my world. But I never want to lose sight of that initial love, purpose, and sense of belonging I found in the water. My therapist reminded me once, two decades after my swimming journey began as I was struggling to stay consistent in showing up to swim each morning, that I seem to be at my best and most confident when I'm on top of my training. In pushing training aside, instead of taking control of managing my schedule better, I was becoming exhausted and skipping the one thing that always helps me. Taking the time to slow down and remember what I enjoy about swimming, and why I do it, helps me to reignite that passion I have for my sport.

I have several friends who have retired from Paralympic swimming and don't even like the idea of swimming anymore. After so many years of dedicating their lives to it, they were ready to be completely done with the sport and never swim another lap again. I never want to get to that place of being so depleted by my sport and the Paralympics that I no longer find any happiness in the water. I want to eventually retire with an immense appreciation for everything swimming has given me, while still accomplishing swim sets on my own to keep my body strong—with no goal but to enjoy gliding through the water and channeling my energy into doing what I love.

As we continue on our journey of self-acceptance, we're going to forget our *why*. We're going to get caught up in the chaos and hold onto the exhaustion or confusion we feel. When this happens, it's so important to take a moment and regroup. When I get tired and frustrated, I do three things to keep myself from getting jaded and bring me back into my *why*.

1. I change my language from "*I have* to do this" to "*I get* to do this."

2. I think back to the beginning, remembering the days when I prayed to be where I am now, and remind myself of how far I've come.

3. I think about what I want my legacy to be.

These three steps are so powerful. I don't *have* to train every day; I *get* to use my body to train every day and strengthen my mind and physique. I don't *have* to travel; I *get* to travel and tell the world my story and the ways God has used my life to make an impact. I *get* to cultivate relationships that challenge and support me. Just this simple shift in language goes hand in hand with being conscious of how I'm talking to myself and what mindset I'm speaking into my life.

What is that thing that you started out of joy or determination and have now perhaps lost sight of for the very reasons you worked so hard for it? Don't keep pushing yourself to give and give if you find yourself stuck in a place where you're depleted. You can't pour from an empty cup. Likewise, you can't give your best if you're burnt out. The next time you're feeling weighed down by your dreams, ask yourself, *Am I practicing a mindset of gratitude and excitement about everything that's in front of me?* When you see your life for the choices you have the *privilege and opportunity* to make each day, rather than for the obligation of having to make those choices, suddenly you see the power that you have through a whole new lens. You can use this new viewpoint to make changes and set boundaries in your schedule where necessary. You *get* to say yes to things, and you can say no to what doesn't serve your end goal.

Go back to the beginning, when your dreams and goals were new and exciting. Take a moment to rekindle that spark of joy you once had. Along with it may come that sense of gratitude that you're no longer where you started but where you set out to be.

MAKE YOUR MARK

As you think about how far you've come, I want you to also think about the *legacy* you want to leave behind. That is such a powerful motivator to me. *What impact am I making? What is the mark that I'd like to leave on the world—and especially on the people closest to me?* Even in the midst of really difficult swim practices, or years where I've considered giving up on swimming, I've always felt that my swimming career was for a bigger purpose. Sure, it also used to be about the medals and sponsorships and adding weight to my voice so I couldn't be ignored. But somewhere deeper, I knew this was bigger than just me.

I've achieved so many of the goals that I set out for myself, but with each achievement comes a reevaluation of my old goals and of the new goals I've yet to set. I never want to stop progressing and challenging myself to be better. Each of us has the capacity for so much, and unfortunately, so many people never reach their full potential. They get to a "good enough" place and then coast through the rest of their lives. As I age into each new season and step toward new goals and challenges, I hope to keep expanding and making an impact. Let your legacy be one of impact as well. As long as you're still here on this earth, you have purpose inside you and something more to give to those around you. How do you want people to remember you?

When I think about legacy, Billie Jean King and the work she is doing through the Women's Sports Foundation comes to mind. I attended my first Women's Sports Foundation gala in 2008, when I was sixteen years old. I wore a purple strapless dress and got to have my hair and makeup done. I was so honored to be invited and to be surrounded by so many incredible women athletes and advocates. I loved meeting Billie Jean King, an American tennis player who fought for equal prize money in the men's and women's games, spearheading the formation of the Women's Tennis Association. It was humbling to connect with athletes like Gabby Douglas and Julie Foudy and to learn more about our fight and history as women in the athletic community. I was nominated a few times for their Sportswoman of the Year award, and though I never won, it was always so powerful just to be in the room, where women champions can celebrate each other. It's not competition, but community. I eventually became part of their Athlete Advisory Panel board and am part of their annual celebration for National Girls and Women in Sports Day.

The Women's Sports Foundation strives to get girls and women active, equipping them to reach their potential in sports and in life. It's through this foundation that I learned about Title IX of the Education Amendments of 1972, which prohibits discrimination based on sex in education programs and activities that receive federal financial assistance. Just a little over fifty years ago, if you were told you couldn't play a sport because they didn't want any girls on the team, there was nothing that gave you any right to fight that. We've come a long way in fifty years. Just imagine what we can do in the next fifty! Imagine what legacy we can leave behind for the next generation.

Rupi Kaur, a Canadian poet, once said in a film called *Rise* (directed by Nisha Ganatra), "And for all the tables that refuse to seat us, we'll build new tables and pull up a seat for everyone who arrives after us."[1]

Because of so many women who stood up and challenged the "rules," I get to pursue this career as a professional swimmer and be part of these incredible communities of women athletes and Paralympic athletes. As you contemplate how far you've come and where you want to go next, consider what tables you've been excluded from and how you're building a space for others who are experiencing the same pushback. How are you creating a space for those *who arrive after you*? This is where all the internal self-work is tested, because it's so much easier to back down and stick to the status quo when we're still stuck in our own shame and unsure of how to use our own voices. But when we're confident in who we are and building from a place of knowing our value and the goals we've laid out before us, we're not afraid to challenge others or experience temporary failure in order to further our legacy for those who come after us. We can see the bigger picture and know what legacy we want to leave behind as we continue to pave the way for future generations.

I've seen changes for the better, even over the course of my own career. The way the Paralympic movement has grown since I was a twelve-year-old girl at my first Paralympic Games gets me even more passionate about where we're headed. When I first became a Paralympian, I knew we were not yet equal with the Olympics. It all felt very separate. No one really knew about the Paralympics, and when I tried to explain the Paralympics to others, they would just end up calling me an Olympian. I didn't correct them, and sometimes I'd just call myself an Olympian, too, because it was easier than explaining and seeing people look less impressed once they realized I didn't compete at the Olympics. Several of my teammates got tattoos of the Olympic rings instead of the Paralympic symbol of the three agitos—swooshes in red, blue, and green, the three colors that are most widely represented in national flags around the world. The five rings were well known, but no one would recognize the three agitos of the Paralympic Games.

I remember being at a Team USA media summit right before the 2008 Olympics and Paralympics, and I was one of only a few Paralympians selected to be there. Allyson Felix (now an eleven-time Olympic gold medalist in track and field) came over and said hi to me and was very welcoming, which made me feel slightly less small and nervous.

I had someone assigned to walk me from interview to interview and help keep me on the schedule I was given. I walked into one of the rooms and told the interviewers that I was a three-time Paralympic gold medalist, training for my second Paralympic Games and that I was seeded first in the world in six events. One woman glanced at me and said, "We don't have any questions for her." I stood there confused for a second, wondering, *Wait, what do you mean?* I came home from the Athens Games with my three gold medals feeling so proud of myself, like I'd accomplished something huge, only to be thrown back into my normal life as a twelve-year-old where no one even knew what the Paralympics were or cared to ask. And there I was at a media summit surrounded by the best athletes in the world, brushed off like they didn't really care either.

I hated feeling that way, and I didn't want any other Paralympians to feel that way. I figured that the more success I had, the more people were going to listen. I decided I was going to win more medals, break world records, and be like Mark Spitz or Michael Phelps. I wanted people to take me more seriously and doubled down on my need to prove my worth by becoming the very best. My determined teenage mind decided that people would know my name, and they'd know what the Paralympics were. I was adamant about making that happen and seeing it take place in my career span, and I knew that we weren't there yet. Sometimes the process over the years has made me angry and tired. But I keep showing up and I keep training and competing and advocating, because I'm seeing the progress and how our voices are starting to be heard.

The Paralympics in Tokyo were the first summer Games where we received the same amount of money for winning a medal that the Olympians receive. Prior to 2018, we earned less than a quarter of the pay that our Olympic counterparts received for each medal. The U.S. Olympic & Paralympic Committee (USOPC) added "Paralympic" to its name in 2019, becoming the first Olympic organization in the world to include Paralympic sports in its official name. The 2014 Sochi Winter Olympics received unprecedented television coverage in the U.S. when NBC Sports partnered with the USOPC (then still called the USOC) for media rights, and we've gotten more and better coverage at each Paralympics since. There's still more to be done, but we're headed in the right direction. We're making a splash (pun intended), and that encourages and excites me!

I've always been proud to be part of Team USA. I worked hard to repeatedly get to wear that swim cap with the American flag on the side and my last name printed underneath it. Having started so young, I grew up in the Paralympics. I went through my teens and my twenties training and swimming professionally, being part of this movement that helped shape my confidence and acceptance of who I am. My journey to grow this sport and grow *within* this sport has called me to continually be involved and active with it. No matter what, I've always felt pulled back to the water and felt that I had more to accomplish here. It *is* part of my legacy.

I was walking through the grocery store, a couple years before writing this, while wearing a Paralympic sweatshirt. Someone walked by me and said, "Oh my gosh, you're in the Paralympics?!"

I smiled and confidently said, "Yes, I am!"

People know what it is now, and it's been so cool getting to see it grow and to see these athletes with such incredible stories of overcoming get the spotlight they deserve. There's a part of me that's sad that I didn't always feel proud enough to call myself a Paralympian, but now I confidently correct people. I am a Paralympian, and that's such an important part of my story and who I am. I love that this is part of my legacy, part of how people will remember me.

GIVING BACK PUSHES US ALL FORWARD TOGETHER

Along with the growth of the Paralympics, we've thankfully seen so much innovation take place in the world of prosthetics. This progression in technology has allowed me to encourage other amputees forward in their journey. It's the comfort and convenience of them that has changed the most over the years. My prosthetics don't fall completely off anymore if someone steps on my foot or if I trip. I have flex ankles that move more like a real ankle would as I walk, instead of offering zero flexibility and shock absorption like my first several pairs of prosthetics did. My legs are shaped out of a lighter carbon fiber material. For my high-heel legs, they took a mold of my sister Hannah's foot in a four-inch arched position and used that to make my legs. Whenever we get dressed up and go out together, we have the same feet!

I still feel pain when I'm exhausted or soreness when I wear my legs all day, but it's so much better than when I couldn't stand for longer than a few minutes without being in pain. With so little bone below my knees,

I don't have a lot to work with in lifting and controlling my prosthetics. My prosthetist, Erik Schaffer, has worked with me for years to get me the best fit that keeps me from hyperextending my knees, pitching my weight forward, or making any adjustments that would eventually impact the rest of my body to compensate for an improper fit. Erik has completely changed my life. A good prosthetist can make such a difference in the life of an amputee. A disability doesn't have to slow you down, and prosthetists help make sure they don't. I can now confidently look into the eyes of an amputee and tell them that it will be okay. So much has improved in magnificent ways, and we will keep pushing forward, both for innovation and equality.

Our world is changing and progressing rapidly, and it's our responsibility to make sure it heads in the right direction. We *get* to challenge ourselves and give back to our communities. We *get* to make an impact in each other's lives as we choose gratitude and build our legacy. Getting to work with the Women's Sports Foundation to empower women, and also teaching young athletes through Fitter & Faster swim clinics, has reminded me how important it is to give back. Advocacy and generosity go hand in hand. When you believe in what you're fighting for, you're more generous with your time, resources, energy, and voice. We can show our support by giving in these areas. This can look like volunteering or financially supporting an organization that is making headway in the area you want to help impact. If you don't know where to start, research and find an organization to donate your time or money to.

I've had the opportunity to donate to a few orphanages over the years—including the one I visited in Russia that was specifically for children with disabilities, and one in India where my grandparents had started an adoption process for two sisters named Linta and Tintu, donating through the nonprofit organization they founded. My husband is a soccer coach, and an organization that is near to our hearts is CP Soccer, which is a competitive league for children affected by cerebral palsy, stroke, and traumatic brain injury. There's also an incredible organization in Baltimore, Maryland, called the Transformation Center; they believe in holistic transformation, and their mission is to "connect people to their God-given destiny by providing the pathways for them to rise above the obstacles of poverty, addiction, poor education, unemployment, and social injustice."[2] Giving back can be done in different ways, but if you have the opportunity and the means to support an already established organization, then do that. No one gets to the end of their life and wishes they had been less generous!

How we're speaking up and giving back, creating change for the better and living a life of generosity . . . that's legacy. That's the impact I want to keep making. I want to continue advocating for equality and visibility, so the next generation doesn't feel alone, so they see all the opportunities laid out in front of them. There are no excuses to not succeed, to not go for what you want, and the only things that can hold us back are our own decisions. That's the level of opportunity we should desire for each and every person. Let's stay grateful and avoid becoming jaded, as we remember where we came from and what we're fighting for. Let's not take anything for granted, because we have purpose and there is more left to do. Because ultimately, it's not even about us—it's about the people whom our actions are impacting. The way we're adding our voices to the thousands that echoed before us—that's something I want to be a part of. I invite you to join in with me.

The Reframe

This week, try implementing in your own life the three habits that I use to help keep me from becoming frustrated or stagnant. Just one week. Just a few gentle reminders as you go throughout your day to help shift your mindset toward one of gratitude and intention. And if you'd like to take it a step further, you can also include the simple gratitude practice each morning and night to really start shifting your mindset.

1. Start changing your language—out loud and internally—from "I *have* to do this" to "I *get* to do this."

2. Think back to the beginning and remind yourself of how far you've come.

3. Think about what you want your legacy to be.

SIMPLE GRATITUDE PRACTICE:

Today I'm grateful for . . .

Try listing three things. This can be as simple as being grateful for your favorite snack—mine is chips and salsa and pickles! Nothing is too small or insignificant.

A good thing that happened to me today was . . .

This is a great exercise to practice at the end of the day. Maybe you got to watch your favorite TV show or spoke with a friend on the phone. Again, nothing is too small or insignificant.

II

Created for Purpose

ONE SUMMER, WHILE I was in Texas with my swim sponsor, Arena, we did a team bonding activity to figure out our core focuses and values as individuals. All twelve of us athletes and the Arena staff were on a getaway weekend where we stayed in a house together. They'd stocked the place with healthy snacks and new Arena gear for each of us, which we were all wearing as we sat around the open living room area. We had a full schedule doing the activities planned out for us, and that evening they had a speaker come from Global Arena to walk us through this exercise. It was something I'd never done before. She stood at the front of the room and asked us, "When you think of a core value, what do you think about?"

We all sat quietly with this question at first, really pondering it, then we talked about it amongst ourselves. In a world that's moving so fast, all we were tasked with doing in that moment was to think about our core values. All we had to do was think, *What are the things I stand for?*

We then passed around a small, black bag filled with various adjectives that represented the different options we could choose from and claim as our own. The speaker told us to pick five words, but we didn't get to look at the words as we chose them. After we got our five words, we had a couple minutes where we could trade words with our peers until we felt we were holding our best five. Even as I reached into the bag to start the exercise, I hoped that my hand wrapped around *purpose*.

A decade and a half after starting my own journey of self-acceptance, I still felt the need to feel that I had a true purpose and to feel grounded in it. I still do. I pulled out the word *courage* but traded that one for *self-love*. We kept trading, and I went through several words, but I finally got my hands on *purpose*. By the end of it, the words in my hands were *purpose, self-control, humility, love,* and *forgiveness*.

My core value and focus has always been centered on living out my purpose in every aspect of my life and also how my purpose could be used to impact others. So feeling this word in my hand felt right. When we were told to eliminate two words from our collection so that we could end up with the most important three words to us, I whittled it down to *purpose, love,* and *forgiveness*. We narrowed it down again so that we all ended up with only one chosen word. Then we had to choose an image out of a selection of pictures and artwork that we felt best represented our top core value and what it meant to us, before giving a mini presentation on our word and image. My core value was purpose, and I chose a picture of a colorful leaf to pair with it. I talked about how life is always changing and we have a purpose in every season. I hold tight to the idea that seasons come and go, but I still hold a power and a purpose in each one.

CHOOSE YOUR IMPACT

The choices you make dictate the impact you create in your life and in others' lives. You are always adding something to the world around you—whether your contributions are positive or negative is up to you.

I have this fear that I'll get to the end of my life and still have so much left to give because I was too selfish or afraid to pour out what I had to offer, instead stifling the fullness of the impact I was designed to make. I don't want to look back on every single moment and think, *Wow, you had so much opportunity. You had so much life. You had so much fight. And you were so caught up in what you didn't have that you failed to see all that you did have. You stayed stagnant and never moved forward.* I don't want us to count ourselves out or withhold what we were placed on this planet to offer. I want us to arrive at the end knowing we have nothing left to give, knowing we used our gifts and passions to impact those around us. I want us to live fully embracing our purposes and helping others to find theirs.

But what exactly *is* purpose? Our purpose is the reason for our existence. It is the joining of your *why*, passions, skills, and experience. I thought I found my purpose in swimming. I thought I found it in championing the Paralympic movement and helping other people with disabilities feel less alone. I thought I found it in church. I thought I found it in giving back to my sport through coaching and sharing my story in public speaking. I think now that it is all of these things. Purpose is finding a need in this world and then filling it. People need an outpouring of genuine love and connection. Fill that need. This world needs individuals who have accepted that they have something to offer and believe it enough to try, to fail, and to keep going. Social systems need to be challenged and changed, and everyone deserves a seat at the table. Kindness and empathy need to be common experiences in all our lives. *Fill those needs.*

Every moment of our lives starts with taking the first step, and walking in our purpose isn't any different. Olympic platform divers didn't start by immediately stepping out onto the ten-meter high dive (comparable to a three-story-high building) and throwing themselves into the air. They had to take many steps and climb many levels of skill and self-confidence to build up to that point, mastering the basics of strength training and correct form, then the springboards, before even starting on the platforms. Before freefalling through the air, executing perfect flips and turns high above the glittering surface of the water, they were learning a beginner's front dive tuck from the lowest springboard. Likewise, excelling in your purpose starts with taking your own very first step: identifying what your life purpose *is*.

We worked through finding our *why* in an earlier chapter, and how identifying that inner motivation is a great place to start in finding what drives your sense of purpose. Think through your own story and what makes you smile. For example, do you love listening to people and solving problems? Does it come naturally to you to make people feel comfortable? Maybe your purpose is to be a nurturer and use that in some capacity to encourage and create community wherever you come across that need. Think about your *why* and also what comes naturally to you. You don't have to force something because it sounds good or it's what other people tell you to do. You know yourself and your passions.

Or maybe think through what makes you angry. I get angry when I feel misunderstood, and that has led me to want to make sure others' voices are heard. Encountering ignorance about disabilities gets me fired up, so I seek to educate. We have the power to take control of our story and use it to bring healing to others, so maybe for you that looks like making sure no one else experiences the abuse or trauma you went through. Maybe you start or join a nonprofit that's making an impact in an area that hurts your heart. What do you feel called to fight for or against? What stands out to you as your *why* or your calling? What do you want to fight for in your life, whether it's a big social issue or a small personal matter? It's in these moments that bring us the most sense of passion and fulfillment that we find what we're meant to do in life.

Looking back on my own life and what has led me to feel like I'm in the right place, both understanding my *why* and checking in with myself on what makes me feel purposeful have been great starting points. They'll also be great building blocks if you're not sure where to begin. When you start thinking about your life, what gets your heart beating fast? What do you get excited about? It could be a certain career field or maybe an idea for a business you've been thinking about starting. It could be cultivating a family that values kindness and lifts each other up. Maybe it's getting involved in your community, hosting your friends and building deep connections, or listening and helping to mentor others in their own journeys. For me, public speaking and motivating others— even by publishing this book—excite me and challenge me. Seeing the impact on others that has come from doing what I love has confirmed for me that I'm in the right place.

OUR DEEPEST VULNERABILITIES CAN
BE OUR STRONGEST WEAPONS

Once you've identified your *why* and feel confident that you've identified at least one purpose you'd like to live toward in your life, then ask yourself, *What makes me feel most vulnerable?* We have to first identify that vulnerability and acknowledge it. When we bury our vulnerable feelings and hide from the areas in our life where we feel different, ashamed, or not good enough, we become unable to fully process and utilize those areas. We must embrace these parts of ourselves and our stories that have the capacity to help guide us to our purpose.

My biggest area of vulnerability is my legs, which is literally the most obvious trait about me that led to me making an impact. Being adopted was another area where I felt deeply vulnerable and insecure. Seeking healing and sharing that vulnerable struggle with others has become another key aspect of my purpose. There are few better feelings for me than having conversations with others who are adopted because I feel understood by them on a whole different level. We all seek to feel understood. It gives us grounding and validation, confidence and self-worth. There are a lot of moments and circumstances in my life that left me feeling misunderstood in my early years through adulthood. When I can relate to someone over our shared experiences, it heals that piece of me that felt misunderstood for so many years. Those areas of vulnerability also give me purpose.

It's the areas in our life where we feel the most vulnerable that can be our greatest weapon and area of impact once we feel confident enough to share them with others. We must each learn to accept and appreciate our differences and the power we have in being unique. All the unique parts make up a collective whole, but if every part looks the same, then what you're building will not be unique to you at all. *You* are the answer to a problem in this world. You are not too much, too weird, too insignificant, too different, or too disabled to fulfill your purpose in this world. In fact, that trait or piece of you that you are ashamed of could turn out to be your greatest asset.

I often think about this little girl I met years ago who lost her leg to cancer. I don't even remember her name, but her parents said she just *had* to meet me. She gazed up at me with so much hope and admiration in her eyes, to see someone else who looked like her to inspire her forward, and that's a moment that will always stick with me. As I've walked through my own ups and downs, it's people like her who make everything feel worth it. I think about the children who wrote school reports on the story of *my* life, and who brought their copies of my first book, *Unsinkable*, with them to my speeches for me to sign. Or the parents who reached out to me on social media to say I helped them understand their child who was adopted or had a disability. Or the grown men and women who've come up to me after some of my speeches to tell me *their* adoption story with tears in their eyes, and how they want to meet their biological moms, too. They all remind me of my purpose here and why I do what I do.

We all have those people in our lives whom we get to impact. Maybe it's your own child absorbing your actions, coworkers who are witnessing how you behave under stress, or friends and family whom you get to encourage and do life with. Whether you realize it or not, you're making an impact in their lives. We each get to decide if we'll walk in our purpose or simply get through each day, doing the minimum for ourselves and those around us.

TO LIVE IN FEAR OR LEARN TO ADJUST

Brené Brown, a research professor, speaker, and author who has spent much of her life studying wholehearted living and the role of courage, vulnerability, shame, and empathy in our lives, focuses on developing theories based on people's lived experiences. Instead of using tests and statistics to measure phenomena, she interviews a diverse group of people about certain subjects or topics and then codes the data, watching for themes to emerge. This is called *qualitative research*. She initially started her research with an interest in the anatomy of human connection. While connection seemed to be what gave life meaning, Brené found herself drawn to how the power of connection in our lives also led to the emergence of fear of disconnection—of being unlovable or unworthy of connection. She later started a study on "wholehearted living," searching for people who were living and loving with their whole hearts even when faced with risk and uncertainty, and seeing what they did differently. In all of her work, she found heavy themes of shame and vulnerability and how that affects our lives, and what she witnessed in the group who were engaging in wholehearted living is that they embraced their vulnerability and imperfections. They allowed themselves the grace to fail, so there was no shame when they did so, and they were able to keep moving forward. According to her research, doing this opens people to love, joy, and belonging by allowing them to know themselves better and to more deeply connect with other people.

When we embrace our vulnerabilities instead of turning to anger or shame, we open ourselves to the very things we are all seeking and were afraid to lose in the first place. Trying to hide or alter ourselves to fit into other people's—or our own—expectations only robs us of the true connection and understanding we seek. We're not weak for struggling, and we're not *less* for being different. When we can shift our mindset about our insecurities and accept all the pieces of ourselves, we too can fully engage in wholehearted living.

Brené writes in one of her books, *Braving the Wilderness*, "True belonging is the spiritual practice of believing in and belonging to yourself so deeply that you can share your most authentic self with the world and find sacredness in both being a part of something and standing alone in the wilderness. True belonging doesn't require you to *change* who you are; it requires you to *be* who you are."[1] We spend so long trying to push down all the parts of ourselves that are different from society's norms or that we believe won't be accepted by others, when we should really be putting that effort into accepting those things about ourselves. If people are accepting a version of you that has been curated and shaved down to fit in, they aren't accepting the authentic you. So, the irony is that only when we can be vulnerable enough to present our true selves to the world can we experience the acceptance that we're seeking.

This is why one of the biggest things that I've seen hold people back from their purpose is fear. We fear failure, looking silly, and exposing our vulnerabilities and areas of weakness. We try so hard to appear like we have it all together, when the truth is that no one does. As soon as we start to get a handle on the circumstances of our life, things change again. That's life. That's growth. That's why we have to be able to accept our vulnerability and move through our fears to see the possibilities.

I've come to understand that we're never done learning and adjusting and growing. I've seen that in my own journey of self-acceptance, as each season brought its own lesson and revelation, and more recently I've seen that physically as I age into being one of the oldest athletes on the U.S. Paralympic swim team.

Turning thirty in 2022 was not something I was initially looking forward to. I know it's not *actually* old, but it made me so aware of the different approach I needed to take in some areas of my life. I want to be able to train like I did at sixteen years old, but in my thirties, I need more recovery time. I spend more time cross-training, doing Pilates and weight training, and paying attention to what feels good in my body as I strengthen it. I also have other areas of my life that matter to me and require my attention outside of swimming. I've had to allow my needs to change with me, my body, and my lifestyle. To be honest, I fought some of those changes initially, but when I tried to push myself mentally and physically while resisting making the adjustments I needed, I only ended up disappointed when I couldn't meet the unrealistic expectations I'd set for myself.

When we fight change, we only end up more stressed, confused, or disappointed. Can you identify an area in your life where you've been resisting change? Pause and really examine why. For a lot of us, it's due to fear. Are you afraid that making a big change won't work out and you'll look ridiculous? Are you afraid that if you slow down, you'll never catch back up to where you want to be? Maybe you've just been doing something one way for so long that you're not even sure how to go about changing or learning a new way.

LISTEN TO YOUR BODY TO HEAL YOUR PAIN

You're going to go through many different seasons. It's only through accepting the season you're in that you can start to adjust to it and move through it. It's only through taking in each new season and seeing what we can learn from it that we can identify our purpose within it. If I were to force myself to keep swimming with my old practices and training the way I used to, my body wouldn't be able to keep up anymore, and I'd end up exhausted or even injured. Likewise, when we resist adjusting to a new season, we end up burnt out and frustrated. We can't step into seasons of grief or pain and carry on acting like everything is fine and happy. We need to allow ourselves to pause, process, and adjust to the changes. When we hold so tightly to the past, we're only ignoring our current reality.

To me, physical training draws a clear parallel to everyday life. Moving through various seasons and accepting them with open arms will help us to thrive within them. When we avoid and ignore, it only makes things worse. I've gone through a few periods of intense shoulder pain and recovery over the years. I kept pushing through and putting my body in pain until I physically couldn't do it anymore. At the point where I was taking the maximum amount of ibuprofen a human could take each day, I finally went to the doctor and got a CT scan. It showed that I had developed arthritis in my shoulders. I had to start adjusting my practices to take care of my body and protect my shoulders. I can't force myself to be the way I was in the past, but I can hold myself accountable to the work I'm putting in now. So can you.

I used to crank out yardage and swim countless laps per practice. Now I do different drills and focus on specific parts of my stroke and how to target and work on certain muscle groups. I do physical therapy, ice my shoulders, use kinesiology therapeutic tape (or k-tape) around my joints, and get massages. I make sure I stretch and warm up my body properly. I use resistance bands and a foam roller, and I always finish my day using my Theragun to help reduce muscle tension and soreness. It was only after I accepted the season I was in, and was honest with myself and others about the care I needed, that I was able to adjust and create a system that worked for me. *Allowing* ourselves to change and adjust with the different seasons that come our way is what will keep us from breaking. I couldn't keep ignoring my reality—I had to listen to my body and respond accordingly.

It's important to learn how to listen to our bodies, in training and in life. We have to learn how to differentiate between when it's time to push ourselves and when it's time to rest. I still sometimes struggle with feeling guilty for taking time to rest, but I've learned that if you don't plan for rest, then your body will force you to rest at some point by getting sick or injured, or just by shutting down in some way. Not showing up because you're mentally stuck—whether out of fear or overthinking—that's the time to push through. When I get stuck, I decide to accomplish one task, even if it's not to perfection. When I feel overwhelmed by how much I need to clean the entire house, I set a thirty-minute timer and only do what I can finish in that time. It saves me from getting too overwhelmed and doing nothing, as well as spending an entire day cleaning to perfection when I'm supposed to be resting or getting something else done. But pushing through when there is physical pain, or when you feel like your brain is shutting down because you're burnt out, is only going to hurt you and add to those feelings. This is where community can come into play, too, because having people who know you and your limits can help you to discern when to push and when to rest.

I'm learning how to communicate those needs, which is how your community will even start to learn your limits. I see too many athletes—and I've gotten that way with coaches in the past as well—who are afraid to take a recovery day or express when they're in pain. As athletes, we're taught to push through the pain. Discomfort and soreness can be pushed through, but actual pain is your body signaling you that something is wrong. As I've gotten older, I'm much more outspoken about what I need. I know my own body better than anyone else, and it's up to me to take care of it. If I need to take a break because my body is older and is giving me signals that I've done enough, then I need to listen to it. If I need a mental health day and to take a moment to reset, I need to listen to that. I'm trying to work out and swim in a way that allows me to have a long swimming career. I'm currently training for the 2024 Paralympic Games in Paris, and I would love to retire at the following Games in Los Angeles, California, on home soil. Our bodies are incredible, and they deserve to be taken care of and spoken up for. It is okay for things to be different, and to still be thankful for how far our bodies have carried us.

No matter what season you're in, you're right on time. This is the perfect time to work on listening to your own needs and making the necessary adjustments to live better, fuller, happier lives. Today is the perfect day to start finding your purpose and who you were meant to impact. Our own purposes within the world have always been within us, waiting to be examined and used to fill a need that this world has. As we start examining what our purposes may be, let's be honest with ourselves about what season we're in and what needs we have. Avoidance and fear only deter us from living in our purposes. Let's continue filling the needs of this world. We're not here to coast through life, untethered to others, but to use our skills and passions and experiences to make a positive impact on ourselves and on others. Dr. Jane Goodall said it best: "You cannot get through a single day without having an impact on the world around you. What you do makes a difference, and you have to decide what kind of difference you want to make."[2]

The Reframe

You build courage every time you move toward what inspires you rather than away from what scares you. So, write a list of everything you'd do if you were not afraid. Write anything and everything that comes to mind. Asking that person out, taking a mental health day at work, posting that poem or video of you singing. . . .

Then start doing the smallest things on your list, and work your way up to the bigger things. Remember that fear itself can't hurt you unless you allow it to keep you from living authentically, speaking truthfully, or doing the things that matter most to you.

Conclusion

I WAS TYPING an email while sitting in the airport when it came to me. It was a line I'd heard dozens of times growing up, and for some reason, it bubbled up to the surface of my mind just when I needed it most. I stopped typing, pausing my fingers over the keys as the simple words settled over me: "You've always had the power, my dear. You just had to learn it for yourself."[1]

The email I was typing, as Glinda the Good Witch's words to Dorothy in *The Wizard of Oz* reverberated inside me, had been a thank-you to my family. It was right before the 2020 Paralympic Games in Tokyo (which ended up taking place in 2021 due to the COVID-19 pandemic), and I hadn't seen my family in a year. I'd gone out to the Olympic and Paralympic Training Center in Colorado Springs as a way to try to catch up on the swimming I'd missed when every pool closed down during the initial COVID outbreak. As things started to reopen, I moved away from my home and my husband, Lucas, in Maryland to focus all my attention on training. I spent a year away from my family under strict regulations at the training center that didn't allow much contact with anyone outside of it, due to extra COVID precautions. I missed my husband and family and wanted to type out some thoughts to share with them, expressing how thankful I was for their constant support. I've never lost sight of the fact that this journey isn't just mine, and every person who has loved and supported me is part of it. They get me through those four years between each Paralympic Games.

I sat there typing out an update and thanking them, and I started to feel nervous because the moment I had been preparing for was finally here—the Tokyo Games. It started to feel real: after one week of training at the Yokota Air Base in western Tokyo, the U.S. Paralympic Team would be ready to move into the Olympic and Paralympic village for the start of competition. I took a deep breath and gave myself an internal pep talk. *Here we go, Jess. You've got this. This is what all the sacrifice and training have been for. You've always had the power, my dear. You just had to learn it for yourself.*

I've always fought to be strong. I've fought to prove myself and show people I belonged. So much of my life has been a fight to accept where I've come from and love myself for every aspect of who I am. I'm still not perfect, but I think I've finally learned that it was never about gaining anyone else's acceptance as much as I needed to gain my own. I've learned that my pain is my own to heal. I've learned that even in accepting the love and grace of God, I still have to apply it to my life and allow it to change me. Real love and forgiveness *affects* us and flows back out of us. It wasn't until I forgave myself that I was able to forgive my mother who gave me up. It wasn't until I embraced my differences and started showing off my legs that I was able to help others to own their own differences. It wasn't until I learned to love myself that I was able to recognize how much power I have to love and impact the world around me.

Whether I'm racing in front of millions of people or I've just jumped in for another swim practice where no one is watching, my worth is no longer something I'm trying to prove. Your worth is not determined by your accomplishments or possessions but by the simple fact that you exist and possess inherent value as a human being. That is our power— that we are here and breathing. This level of self-love is the foundation of a fulfilling life, because it allows you to treat yourself with kindness, compassion, and understanding, thereby creating a harmonious relationship with yourself and the world around you.

The only constant in life is change, and throughout my life, I've learned that our worth does not fluctuate with our circumstances. It does not change with who is in our life or with what people say about us. It isn't based on what we accomplish or how many medals and awards we win. But we have to believe that for ourselves, and *that* can be the challenging part. So many people, including other para-athletes, have asked me how I've become successful and what steps I took to get there. The first question I ask them in return is, "Well, do you believe in yourself?"

Our own beliefs about ourselves and the world directly impact every area of our lives. It's okay if you're not all the way there yet, fully believing in yourself in every moment, but I believe that one day you will stop striving for the approval of others and start believing in your own worth and purpose. There have been so many moments where I've struggled to believe in myself. I've felt powerless in my adoption and with missing my legs. Yet, the realization of my own choices and responsibility to heal, to live with gratitude, and to keep showing up every day has revealed to me the power I *do* have.

I am not a victim to my circumstances, and neither are you. Those words spoken by Glinda the Good Witch in *The Wizard of Oz* nudge me to keep moving forward, through the ups and downs, and keep believing in the work I'm doing and the impact I'm having on the world around me. I picture my younger self—little Jess—looking me in the eyes and encouraging me, "You've always had the power." You just have to remember it, or find it, or believe it for yourself. When seasons of doubt come—where you're feeling unsure and unsteady—remember there's a younger version of yourself who still believes in you. There's something about this that's comforting and reassuring to me, something about it that gives me peace, encouraging me to keep going. Even in the moments we don't see it yet, all of our choices and actions are making an impact, either on others or on ourselves. If we remain patient and consistent in our goals, we will see change start to take shape. And even when we're close to giving up, if you can impact one person, that right there is enough.

My life is riddled with stories and moments where I've struggled to come to this place of self-acceptance. But ultimately this journey has made me stronger and given me more compassion and the ability to connect with others through my platform. Sharing my story, including the ugly and uncomfortable parts, will hopefully give you the courage to share your own. Your voice deserves to be heard, even if it shakes when you speak. And as we each start sharing our experiences and normalizing our differences, we will find that we're actually incredibly similar—that our differences and vulnerabilities are what connect us.

True self-acceptance lies in embracing all aspects of who you are, including your flaws and imperfections, and recognizing that they are integral parts of your unique identity and humanity. I've seen the impact of the difference it makes to embrace who we are and find the power in our differences. Our power is within us, and it's up to us to utilize that power to make our world better. This all starts from a place of self-acceptance. I've watched it happen in my own life and in the lives of those closest to me. Stepping into our purpose, fully loving and accepting who we are and what we have to offer, is how we reach our full potential and become leaders and world-changers. It's also how we find a sense of peace within ourselves. We can spend our entire lives searching for purpose and meaning, striving to achieve to be worthy, when our purpose has actually been within us all along. No matter what season you're in, you're not alone, and each of us has the ability to make a difference. Starting now. Let's take the first step.

After all, "You've always had the power, my dear." Just click your heels and believe.

Acknowledgments

THERE WAS A time I thought I could never talk about these things or share so vulnerably. I'm endlessly grateful for the people in my life, as well as the team behind this book, who have helped me walk through this lifelong process.

First, I want to thank Hannah, my little sister and writer. The person I trust with all my inner thoughts, who knows how to see my heart and write it out exactly how I want to express it. She knows all my secrets and lived so much of this journey right by my side. I knew it had to be her to write my story. I'm so thankful for her wisdom as she helped me work through my childhood feelings, often getting a call from me immediately following my therapy sessions. I love you always, H.

To Jaime and the amazing team at Sounds True. I cannot thank you all enough for giving me this platform to share my story. You have given me the freedom to share with the world all the parts of myself that I hid away for so long. You have worked tirelessly to help me create something that truly feels like me. Jaime, you were the positive light we all needed during this process.

My amazing editors, Felice and Diana, cultivated a safe space to collaborate and made me feel heard. Felice was the breath of fresh air when my thoughts didn't make sense or I felt stuck, and Diana's excitement about this project renewed my own. Thank you both for handling my thoughts and feelings with gentleness.

I have the absolute best sports agent and am so glad he came into my life when he did. Ian, thank you for keeping me focused and pushing me to keep reaching higher and dreaming bigger for my future. Your work is always appreciated.

My parents deserve the world. They have unwaveringly supported me and believed in my dreams alongside me. When I doubted myself, they encouraged me and held space for me. When I felt like a failure, they reminded me that my worth was not in swimming and that I was a person outside of that. Thank you, Mom and Dad, for teaching me what unconditional love looks like.

A big thank-you to my husband, Lucas, for always believing in me, dreaming with me, and bringing me my iced coffee in the mornings. We have gone through so many seasons together, and you hold my whole heart. I love you forever.

I can't thank my therapist enough. Bethany listens and challenges me in all the right ways, and she has helped me to own the power in all the facets of who I am. Thank you for encouraging me to dig deeper. Putting in the work in our sessions ultimately allowed this book to come to life.

And last but certainly not least, I thank Jesus for showing me what true peace and belonging look like. I wholeheartedly believe that God has been by my side through every part of my life. Every obstacle and difficult circumstance has *still* led to beauty and opportunity when placed in His loving hands. He takes what was shattered and makes it new.

Notes

CHAPTER 1: THE FIRST RIPPLES OF OTHERNESS

1. Dario Cvencek, Anthony G. Greenwald, and Andrew N. Meltzoff, "Implicit Measures for Preschool Children Confirm Self-Esteem's Role in Maintaining a Balanced Identity," *Journal of Experimental Social Psychology* 62 (January 2016): 50–57, doi.org/10.1016/j.jesp.2015.09.015.

2. "Competitiveness," The Child Psychology Service CIC, accessed August 8, 2023, thechildpsychologyservice.co.uk/advice-strategy/competitiveness.

3. "Understanding the Stress Response," Harvard Health Publishing, (July 6, 2020). last updated April 3, 2024, health.harvard.edu/staying-healthy/understanding-the-stress-response.

4. Bessel A. van der Kolk, *The Body Keeps the Score: Brain, Mind, and Body in the Healing of Trauma* (New York: Viking, 2014), 21.

CHAPTER 3: ACCEPTANCE OR AVOIDANCE?

1. Mayo Clinic Staff, "Stress Symptoms: Effects on Your Body and Behavior," Mayo Foundation for Medical Education and Research August 10, 2023, mayoclinic.org/healthy-lifestyle/stress-management/in-depth/stress-symptoms/art-20050987.

CHAPTER 4: TWO WORLDS COLLIDE

1. Kimberly A. Powell and Tamara D. Afifi, "Uncertainty Management and Adoptees' Ambiguous Loss of Their Birth Parents," *Journal of Social and Personal Relationships* 22, no. 1 (February 2005): 129–151, doi.org/10.1177/0265407505049325.

2. David M. Brodzinsky, Marshall D. Schechter, and Robin Marantz Henig, *Being Adopted: The Lifelong Search for Self* (New York: Doubleday, 1992).

3. A. Brown, C. S. Waters, and K. H. Shelton, "A Systematic Review of the School Performance and Behavioural and Emotional Adjustments of Children Adopted from Care," *Adoption & Fostering* 41, no. 4 (2017): 346–368, doi.org/10.1177/0308575917731064.

4. Karla McLaren, *The Language of Emotions: What Your Feelings Are Trying to Tell You* (Boulder: Sounds True 2023).

CHAPTER 6: THE MEASURE OF SUCCESS

1. Erma Bombeck, via Legacy Creative [rom], accessed August 8, 2023, legacycreative.com/2022/08/erma-bombeck/.

CHAPTER 8: REDEFINING SOCIETY

1. "Disability," World Health Organization March 7, 2023, who.int/news-room/fact-sheets/detail/disability-and-health.

2. Matthew F. Garnett, Sally C. Curtin, and Deborah M. Stone, "Suicide Mortality in the United States, 2000–2020," NCHS Data Brief, no. 433 (Hyattsville, MD: National Center for Health Statistics, 2022), dx.doi.org/10.15620/cdc:114217.

3. Angela M. Griffin and Judith H. Langlois, "Stereotype Directionality and Attractiveness Stereotyping: Is Beauty Good or Is Ugly Bad?" *Social Cognition* 24, no. 2 (April 2006):187–206, dx.doi.org/10.1521/soco.2006.24.2.187.

4. Rod Hollier, "Physical Attractiveness Bias in the Legal System," The Law Project, March 14, 2017, thelawproject.com.au/insights/attractiveness-bias-in-the-legal-system.

CHAPTER 9: REPRESENTATION MATTERS

1. Division of Cancer Epidemiology & Genetics Staff, "Neurodiversity," National Cancer Institute, April 25, 2022, https://dceg.cancer.gov/about/diversity-inclusion/inclusivity-minute/2022/neurodiversity,
2. Jane Goodall and Douglas Abrams, *The Book of Hope: A Survival Guide for an Endangered Planet* (New York: Celadon Books 2021).

CHAPTER 10: IN THE NAME OF LEGACY

1. *Rise*, directed by Nisha Ganatra (Los Angeles, CA: Hello Sunshine, 2023), 8 minutes.
2. The Transformation Center website, accessed August 8, 2023, transformationcenter.tc/about.

CHAPTER 11: CREATED FOR PURPOSE

1. Brené Brown, *Braving the Wilderness: The Quest for True Belonging and the Courage to Stand Alone* (New York: Random House, 2017), 40.

CONCLUSION

1. *The Wizard of Oz*, directed by Victor Fleming (Beverly Hills, CA: Metro-Goldwyn-Mayer, 1939), 1 hour, 42 minutes.

About the Author

JESSICA LONG IS one of America's most decorated athletes of all time. She has earned a collection of 29 Paralympic swimming medals, a number she plans on adding to at the upcoming 2024 Paralympic Games; is a world record holder in several events; is a four-time ESPY Award winner; and was listed in *Forbes* 30 Under 30 in 2018. You can watch her 2021 Toyota Super Bowl commercial, titled "Upstream," online. Jessica is a speaker, author, advocate, and sports personality who focuses on succeeding in the water and inspiring others outside the pool. She currently lives in Maryland with her husband, Lucas, and their dog, Goose. Connect with her at jessicalong.com or on social media @jessicatatianalong.

About Sounds True

SOUNDS TRUE WAS founded in 1985 by Tami Simon with a clear mission: to disseminate spiritual wisdom. Since starting out as a project with one woman and her tape recorder, we have grown into a multimedia publishing company with a catalog of more than 3,000 titles by some of the leading teachers and visionaries of our time, and an ever-expanding family of beloved customers from across the world.

In more than three decades of evolution, Sounds True has maintained our focus on our overriding purpose and mission: to wake up the world. We offer books, audio programs, online learning experiences, and in-person events to support your personal growth and awakening, and to unlock our greatest human capacities to love and serve.

At SoundsTrue.com you'll find a wealth of resources to enrich your journey, including our weekly *Insights at the Edge* podcast, free downloads, and information about our nonprofit Sounds True Foundation, where we strive to remove financial barriers to the materials we publish through scholarships and donations worldwide.

To learn more, please visit SoundsTrue.com/freegifts or call us toll-free at 800.333.9185.

Together, we can wake up the world.